Ernest Alfred W. Budge

The Dwellers on the Nile

Chapters on the life, literature, history and customs of the ancient Egyptians

Ernest Alfred W. Budge

The Dwellers on the Nile
Chapters on the life, literature, history and customs of the ancient Egyptians

ISBN/EAN: 9783337330330

Printed in Europe, USA, Canada, Australia, Japan

Cover: Foto ©Andreas Hilbeck / pixelio.de

More available books at **www.hansebooks.com**

By-Paths of Bible Knowledge.

VIII.

THE DWELLERS ON THE NILE

OR

CHAPTERS ON THE LIFE LITERATURE HISTORY AND CUSTOMS OF THE ANCIENT EGYPTIANS.

BY

E. A. WALLIS BUDGE, M.A.

CHRIST'S COLLEGE, CAMBRIDGE.

Assistant in the Department of Oriental Antiquities, British Museum.
Author of 'Babylonian Life and History.'

THE RELIGIOUS TRACT SOCIETY,

56, PATERNOSTER ROW ; 65, ST. PAUL'S CHURCHYARD.

1885.

And the spirit of Egypt shall fail in the midst thereof ; and I will destroy the counsel thereof : and they shall seek to the idols, and to the charmers, and to them that have familiar spirits, and to the wizards.

And the waters shall fail from the sea, and the river shall be wasted and dried up.

And they shall turn the rivers far away ; and the brooks of defence shall be emptied and dried up : the reeds and flags shall wither.

The paper reeds by the brooks, by the mouth of the brooks, and every thing sown by the brooks, shall wither, be driven away, and be no more.

The fishers also shall mourn, and all they that cast angle into the brooks shall lament, and they that spread nets upon the waters shall languish.

Moreover they that work in fine flax, and they that weave networks, shall be confounded.

And they shall be broken in the purposes thereof, all that make sluices and ponds for fish.

Surely the Princes of Zoan are fools, the counsel of the wise counsellors of Pharaoh is become brutish : how say ye unto Pharaoh, I am the son of the wise, the son of ancient kings ?

The Princes of Zoan are become fools, the Princes of Noph are deceived.

Isaiah xix.

CONTENTS.

———

A 2

CHAPTER IV.

ILLUSTRATIONS OF THE PENTATEUCH AND BIBLE PASSAGES FROM THE EGYPTIAN MONUMENTS.

CHAPTER V.

EGYPTIAN LITERATURE.

CHAPTER VI.

THE EGYPTIAN RELIGION.

CHAPTER VII.

THE BURIAL OF THE DEAD.

CONTENTS.

CHAPTER VIII.

THE MUMMY.

CHAPTER IX.

THE BOOK OF THE DEAD.

CHAPTER X.

THE LIFE OF THE ANCIENT EGYPTIANS.

CHAPTER XI.

ARCHITECTURE AND ART.

APPENDIX.

LIST OF ILLUSTRATIONS.

—→←—

INTRODUCTION.

THE land of Egypt, its people and their history, have been the subjects of the most earnest enquiry both in ancient and modern times. The reason is not far to seek, for apart from its importance to the philologist and profane historian, the nation claims the attention of every Bible reader and student, from the fact of its being contemporary with Abraham, and the nursing land of the Jewish nation. When the patriarch Abraham found a famine in Canaan, he sought food and life in the land of the Pharaohs; and after Joseph had become 'the ruler of the land,' Jacob journeyed thither that his posterity might fill the measure of their four hundred (or four hundred and thirty) years' captivity. The Jews entered the land 'when they were but a few men in number,' they went out by myriads; they went in as visitors dependent on the good favour of the Pharaoh, they went out with triumph. Egypt was a place of refuge alike for the founder of the race, for the families of the patriarchs, and for their mighty Descendant, 'The Giver of Life,' Who with His mother departed by night into Egypt.

The influence of the Egyptians upon the Jews was

marked and powerful, and there can be no doubt that
living for so long a time in a land where civilization had
been known for thousands of years, where learning in
all its branches was studied and cultivated, and where
there was a luxurious and polished system of life, with
its magnificent temples and buildings and worship,
must have influenced Israel in its infancy for good and
for bad.   In a good way the influence would show itself
by the Jews gathering to themselves some of the learning
and wisdom for which the Egyptians were famed among
the nations around.   The Egyptian education of Moses
was never forgotten by the posterity of Abraham, for
the martyr Stephen in his dying speech remembered
that Moses 'was learned in all the wisdom of the
Egyptians.' Much else too would they learn of the
arts of the Egyptians : the dyeing of skins, the weaving of
cloth, the cutting of precious stones, and the manufacture
of ' fine twined linen wrought with needlework,' etc. All
this knowledge was put to a glorious use later on in the
making of the Tabernacle and the instruments for its
service. The whole description of the Tabernacle in
Exodus is full of allusions to Egyptian customs : the
strict rules for the purifying of the priests, the ephod of
the high-priest, the pomegranate decoration of the hem
of his robe, his breast-plate and his mitre, all had their
counterpart among the Egyptians. And not only was the
knowledge gained from the Egyptians sanctified to the
service of the Lord, but the mirrors which the Israelitish
women possessed, and which had been brought by them

from Egypt, were melted down and went to make the
'laver of brass and the foot of it.'[1]   Recently, Renouf
has shown that the word *cherubim* may have been derived
from the Egyptian *cherefu*.   The evil effects of the stay
of the Hebrews in Egypt are best shown by the
readiness with which they worshipped the 'golden calf,'
or Apis, set up by Aaron during the absence of Moses ;
and when difficulties met them and food was scarce, by
their demoralised proneness to return to Egypt, where,
though in a state of servitude, they had enjoyed an abundance of cucumbers, melons, leeks, onions, and garlic.

Before the present century every writer on Egypt was
compelled to rely upon the statements of Greek and
other historians, who not only often misunderstood what
they were told, but filled up their works in many places
with obsolete traditions and their own ideas.   The day for
this necessity, however, is now past, and though there
are many difficulties yet to be overcome in the Egyptian
language, still enough has been made out to show how
carelessly the religion and customs of the Egyptians
have been represented by foreign writers.   Pyramid and
obelisk, sarcophagus and coffin, stele and papyrus and
leather have now spoken, and their inscriptions, ranging
from 4000 B.C. to the time of Christ, have in a great
measure yielded up the authentic history of the dwellers
by the Nile ; and its real bearing on the civilization of
the West, extending even to our own times, is now
beginning to be rightly appreciated.

[1] Exodus xxxviii. 8.

The mere names of the works on Egypt would fill a
large book, but a strong line of demarcation must
be drawn between those published before and after the
year 1817. Before that time Egypt was the subject
of the wildest theories and conjectures, but after
Champollion's discovery of the true reading of the
hieroglyphs and their meaning, this was no longer
possible; theory vanished before fact, and conjecture
before certain knowledge.

In the following pages an attempt has been made to
give a very brief sketch of a few of the principal events
in the history of Egypt (especially the part relating to
the Bible narratives of Joseph and of Moses), its people
their mode of life and literature, etc.   But I wish it to be
distinctly understood that I am well aware how impossible
it is even to touch upon all the important heads of so
vast a subject in a little book like this.

The information here given has been obtained from
the first and best sources.   For the history of the
decipherment of the hieroglyphs I have relied upon
that of Dr. Birch, published in the late Sir Gardner
Wilkinson's 'The Egyptians in the time of the Pharaohs,'
London, 1857.   Considering that this is the only good
and trustworthy account of this matter in England, I
wonder much that no one has considered it worth
while to reprint Dr. Birch's part of that work.   The
greater part of Egyptian history has been long well
known, and the principal books consulted by me for the
history of Egypt were 'Egypt,' by Dr. Birch, in the

'Ancient History from the Monuments' series; Wiedemann's 'Aegyptische Geschichte,' and Brugsch's 'Egypt
under the Pharaohs.' A long array of books and papers
in the 'Transactions' of the learned Societies constitute
the authorities for the remaining chapters of the book ;
and I am glad to express my obligations to their authors,
more especially to Dr. Birch, Mr. Le Page Renouf,
and Messrs. Stern, Brugsch, Maspero, Naville, Wilkinson, and Wiedemann.

My thanks are also due to Dr. Garnett of the British
Museum for his care and kindness in reading the proof
sheets.

Chronological Table of the Principal Kings of Egypt, with approximate Dates.[1]

1st Dynasty.	B.C.			B.C.
Menã...	4400	Chã-f-Rã		3666
Ṭetà	4366	Men-kau-Rã...		3633
Ãtet	4333	Shepseskaf		3600
Ãta	4300			
Hesep-ti ...	4266	**5th Dynasty.**		
Mer-bapen ...	4233			
Semenptaḥ ...	4200	Userkaf		3566
Kebḥ...	4166	Sahu-Rã		3533
		Kaka...		3500
		Nefer-Rã		3466
2nd Dynasty.		Rã-en-user-Ãn		3433
		Menkau-Her		3400
Bet'au ...	4133	Ṭet-ka-Rã		3366
Kakau ...	4100	Unas...		3333
Ba-neter-en ...	4066			
Uaínes ...	4033			
Senṭà... ...	4000	**6th Dynasty.**		
		User-ka-Rã		3300
3rd Dynasty.		Tetà		3266
		Meri-Rã		3233
Tatai	3966	Meren-Rã		3200
Nebka	3933	Nefer-ka-Rã		3166
T'er-sa	3900	Mer-en-Rã-Ment-em-saf ...		3133
Tetà	3866			
Setes	3833	**7th–11th Dynasties.**		
Ra-nefer-ka	3800			
		Neter-ka-Rã...		3100
4th Dynasty.		Men-ka-Rã		3066
		Nefer-ka-Rã...		3033
Snefru	3766	Nefer-ka-Rã Nebi		3000
Chufu	3733	Ṭet-ka-Ra-maã-kes (?) ...		2966
Rã-ṭeṭ-f	3700	Nefer-ka-Rã Chentu ...		2933

[1] The dates are those of Brugsch, as published in 'Egypt under the Pharaohs,' ii., p. 311.

	B.C.
Mer-en-Her	2900
Senefer-ka	2866
Rā-en-ka	2833
Nefer-ka-Rā Tererl	2800
Nefer-ka-Her	2766
Nefer-ka-Rā Pepi-seneb ...	2733
Nefer-ka-Rā Annu	2700
. . . . . . kau-Rā ...	2666
Nefer-kau-Rā	2633
Nefer-kau-Her	2600
Neferárka-Rā	2566
Neb-cher-Rā	2533
Seānchka-Rā	2500

12th Dynasty.

Amenemḥā I.	2466
Usertsen I.	2433
Amenemḥā II.	2400
Usertsen II.	2366
„ III.	2333
Amenemḥā III.	2300
„ IV.	2266

13th–17th Dynasties.

Here comes a break of 500 years, in which the 'Shepherd Kings' rule falls.

18th Dynasty.

Àḥmes	1700
Àmenḥetep I.	1666
Thothmes I.	1633
„ II. „ III. ...	1600
Àmenḥetep II.	1566
Thothmes IV.	1533
Àmenḥetep III.	1500
Her-em-ḥeb	1466
Heretic kings	1433

	B.C.
19th Dynasty.	
Rāmeses I. ...	1400
Seti I. ...	1366
Rāmeses II.	1333
Merenptah ...	1300
Seti II. ...	1266
20th Dynasty.	
Setnecht, Rāmeses III.	1233
Rāmeses III. ...	1200
„ IV. „ V. „ VI. „ VII. „ VIII.	1166
„ IX. „ X. „ XI. „ XII. „ XIII.	1133
21st Dynasty.	
Herḥer	1100
Piankhi	1066
Pi-net'em	1033
Pa-seb-chā-nen I.	1000
Men-cheper-Rā	—
Amen-em-àp-t	—
Pa-seb-chā-nen II. ...	—
22nd Dynasty.	
Sheshank I.	966
Osorkon I.	933
Takelot I.	900
Osorkon II.	866
Sheshank II.	833
Takelot II.	800
Sheshank III.	—
Pimai	—
Sheshank IV.	—

	B.C.
23rd Dynasty.	
Pet-tu-Bast	—
Osorkon III. ...	766

	B.C.
24th Dynasty.	
Bak-en-ren-f...	733

	B.C.
25th Dynasty.	
Shabaka ⎫	
Shabataka ⎬ ...	700
Taharka	693

	B.C.
26th Dynasty.	
Psamtek I. ...	666
Nekau ...	612
Psamtek II....	596
Uah-âb-Râ ...	591
Åhmes II. ...	572
Psamtek III.	528

	B.C.
27th Dynasty.	
Cambyses	527
Darius I.	521
Xerxes I.	486

	B.C.
Artaxerxes	465
Xerxes II.	- -
Sogdianus	—
Darius II.	424

	B.C.
28th Dynasty.	
Amen-rut (Amyrtaeus)	—

	B.C.
29th Dynasty.	
Nai-f-āa-u-rut I.	399
Muthes	—
Pa-sa-Mut	—
Nai-f-āa-u-rut II.	379

	B.C.
30th Dynasty.	
Necht-Her-heb	378
Teher	360
Necht-neb-f (Nectanebus) ...	358

	B.C.
31st Dynasty.	
Ochus	340
Arses...	338
Darius III.	336
Conquest by Alexander the Great	332

THE DWELLERS ON THE NILE,

OR,

CHAPTERS ON THE LIFE, LITERATURE, HISTORY, AND CUSTOMS OF THE ANCIENT EGYPTIANS.

———✱———

CHAPTER I.

DECIPHERMENT OF THE EGYPTIAN HIEROGLYPHICS.

AMONG the many linguistic triumphs which have been achieved by scholars in the nineteenth century, the decipherment of the cuneiform inscriptions[1] and the Egyptian hieroglyphics takes the foremost place. By their decipherment two of the greatest and most important nations of antiquity have had their proper place assigned to them among the nations of the past, and what is still better and of more use, their history has been unfolded and their learning and wisdom made available for the people of to-day. Egypt, and its people, whose past extends through a vista of sixty or seventy centuries, have ever been the subject of

[1] For a popular and interesting account of the decipherment of the cuneiform inscriptions, see Prof. Sayce, 'Fresh Light from the Ancient Monuments,' pp. 10–20.

misunderstanding and of misrepresentation. The highly
cultivated nations that flourished about the period of
Egypt's final decay despised its religion, and invented a
variety of absurd statements to cover their ignorance
of a subject which they did not understand. But
now there is neither room nor need for conjecture or
hypothesis, for, thanks to the labour of Egyptologists,
the native Egyptian records have been forced to yield
up their secrets, and we have the means of judging
for ourselves what their language, literature, and
religion were like.

It must not be imagined for a moment that everything
relating to the Egyptians is known, for it is not. Much
has still to be done in many branches of the science.
Travellers who visit Egypt year by year see each time
antiquities and ruins that they have never seen before,
and tell us that in spite of the magnificent collections
of Egyptian antiquities in London, Paris, Turin, Berlin,
Boulak, and elsewhere, Egypt is only half excavated, and
that as much, if not more, exists under the ground as
above it. What has already been found will serve as a
specimen of what is still to be found; so likewise
what Egyptologists have already made out from the
monuments and papyri is but an earnest of what is yet
to come.

Before going further, however, it will be convenient
here to relate briefly the story of the decipherment of the
Egyptian hieroglyphics.[1] The man to whom the world

[1] For the history of this triumph, and for a list of the writers on

principally owes its gratitude for this work is Champollion. As might be expected, one of the most serious difficulties to be overcome before any good work could be done in the way of reading the Egyptian hieroglyphics, was to obtain careful and accurate copies of inscriptions. Many scholars like Kircher, and travellers like Pococke, published copies of inscriptions, but the characters were so distorted and badly drawn that they were worthless for the purpose of reading or study. Many attempts had been made to read the hieroglyphics in the sixteenth century, but no real progress was made ; and in the seventeenth century Athanasius Kircher published his 'Œdipus Ægyptiacus;' in which he professed to give translations of Egyptian stelæ and also of an obelisk. It is perhaps needless to say that his principles of decipherment were absolutely worthless, and it is quite clear that he did not understand that some of the signs represented letters. He considered each sign to represent an idea, and, as Dr. Birch has pointed out,[1] he translated Domitian's title *Autocrator*, by 'the author of fruitfulness and of all vegetation is Osiris, whose productive force was produced in his kingdom of heaven through the holy Mophta.'

The first three-quarters of the eighteenth century also saw much valuable time and learning wasted in

Egyptian, ancient and modern (up to 1857), see the 'Introduction to the Study of the Egyptian Hieroglyphs,' by Dr. Birch, in Wilkinson's 'The Egyptians in the Time of the Pharaohs.'

[1] Wilkinson, 'The Egyptians in the Time of the Pharaohs,' p. 191.

producing works on the Egyptian hieroglyphics which
were productive of no good results; but in the fourth
quarter some facts were made out which served to
hasten the solution of the difficult problem of decipherment.   De Guignes found out that groups with
determinative characters existed in Egyptian, and
Zoega made two startling discoveries, (1) that the hieroglyphs were letters; (2) that each *cartouche* contained a
royal name,[1] though this latter discovery was also made
independently by Thomas Young.   These were the first
steps made in the right direction.

Matters remained thus until the French scientific
expedition to Egypt under Napoleon I. took place.   In
1799 an artillery officer named Boussard discovered,
while digging the foundation of a house at Fort St.
Julien, near Rosetta, the ancient Bolbitane, a large
black stone, which has since been generally called the
'Rosetta Stone,' and which is now in the British
Museum.   It stood originally in a temple of the god
Tmu, and was presented to the French Institute of
Cairo: it was afterwards surrendered to General
Hutchinson, and was presented by George III. to the
British Museum.[2]

Now, to understand an unknown language it is
necessary to have an interpreter, and, as Champollion

[1] The names of kings, queens, and princes are enclosed in ovals, to which
the name *cartouche* has been given: thus (□ ‖ 𓀀 ☰) 'Psammetichus.'

[2] Wilkinson, ' The Egyptians in the Time of the Pharaohs,' p. 192.

B 2

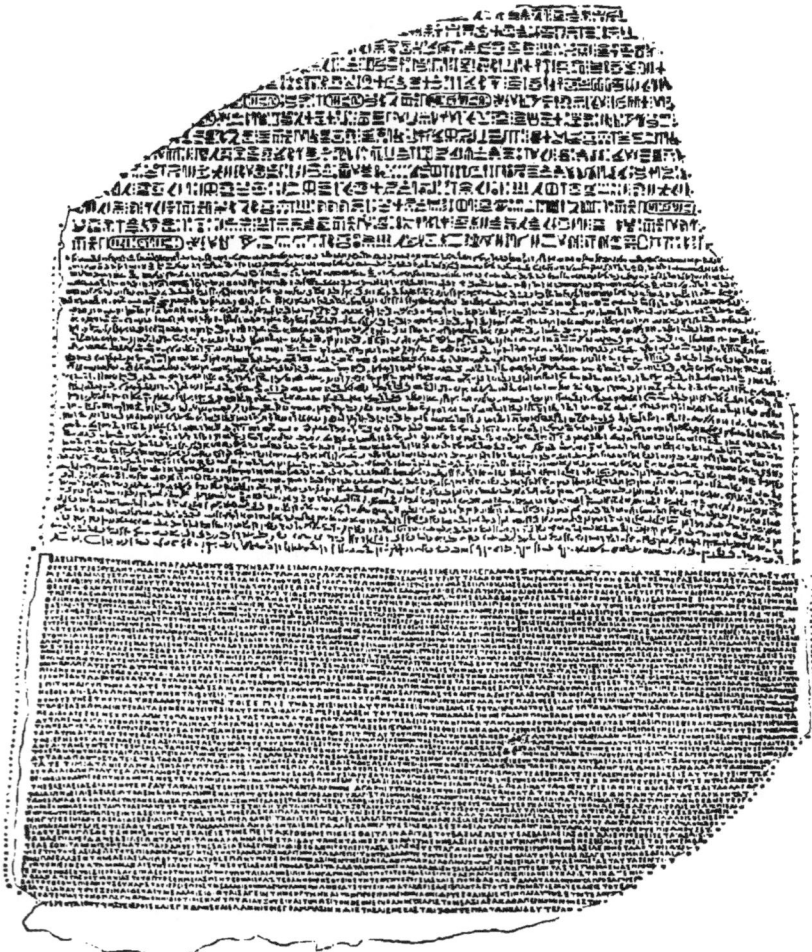

Fac-Simile of Inscriptions on Rosetta Stone.

has said,[1] the interpreter must be either a man, or a book, or a writing; in this case the unknown language was Egyptian, and the interpreter was the writing on the Rosetta Stone. The stone is three feet two inches long, two feet five inches wide, and contains inscriptions in three kinds of writing : one in hieroglyphics, another in demotic, or the language of the people, and the third in Greek. Most unfortunately a very large piece of the end of the stone containing the hieroglyphic part of the inscription was broken away, but enough remained for the purposes of interpretation. Scholars saw immediately that a key was at hand for the unlocking of the mysteries of the Egyptian language, and renewed their studies with great vigour. A fac-simile of the inscription on the stone was made by the Society of Antiquaries in 1802, and distributed among scholars ; and for the first time a scientific attempt was made to translate Egyptian.

When the Greek text of the inscription had been read, it was found that it was a decree drawn up by the priests of Memphis in honour of their king Ptolemy Epiphanes, B.C. 198, who had conferred enormous benefits upon them, and they in gratitude had enjoined that ' this decree should be engraved on a tablet of hard stone, in hieroglyphical, enchorial, and Greek characters, and should be set up in each of the first, second, and third rate temples, at the statue of the ever-living king.'

Since the Rosetta Stone has always been an object of

[1] ' L'Univers,' p. 222.

the greatest curiosity to those who are interested in the history of Egyptian decipherment, we reproduce here a complete translation of it by Dr. Birch. As the hieroglyphic text is imperfect, and the demotic not yet fully translated, the translation here given is from the Greek. It was first published by Dr. Birch in Arundale and Bonomi's 'Gallery of Antiquities,' p. 114; and afterwards in 'Records of the Past,' Vol. IV., pp. 69–78. We must add, however, that last December the Museum of Boulak bought a stele, found at En-Nobeireh near Damanour, which contained a duplicate copy of the text inscribed upon the Rosetta Stone. A reproduction of the stele and the text is given by Urbain Bouriant in the 'Recueil de Travaux relatifs à la Philologie et à l'Archéologie Égyptiennes et Assyriennes,' Paris, 1885.

TRANSLATION OF THE ROSETTA STONE.

Under the reign of YOUTH, and immediate successor of his father, lord of the diadems, very glorious; having established order in Egypt; pious towards the gods; superior to his adversaries; having ameliorated the life of men; Master of the festivals of thirty years, like Hephaistos the Great; like the Sun great king of the Upper and Lower regions; born of the gods Philopatores, approved by Hephaistos; to whom the sun has given victory; living image of Zeus; Son of the Sun, Ptolemy, always living, beloved of Ptah, the ninth year; Aetes son of Aetes, being Priest of Alexander and of the gods Soteres and of the gods Adelphoi, and of the gods Euergetai, and of the gods Philopatores, and of the god Epiphanes, Eucharistes, Pyrrha, daughter of Philinos, being the *Athlophoros* of Berenice

Euergetes, Aria daughter of Diogenes; being the *Kanephoros* of Arsinoë Philadelphos Eirene, daughter of Ptolemy; being Priestess of Arsinoë Philopator on the 4th of the month χandikos; and the 18th of the month of the Egyptians, Mechir (March)

A Decree.

The high priests and prophets, and those who go into the sanctuary for the clothing of the gods, and feather-bearers and sacred scribes, and all the other priests, who from the temples of the country had assembled at Memphis, before the King, at the festival of the reception of the crown, of Ptolemy, ever living, beloved of Ptah, the god Epiphanes, Eucharistes, which he received direct from his father, assembled in the temple at Memphis, this same day, have said: 'Inasmuch as King Ptolemy, ever living, beloved of Ptah, god Epiphanes, Eucharistes, issue of the King Ptolemy and of the Queen Arsinoë, gods Philopatores, has filled the temples with benefactions and those therein dwelling, and all those who are placed under his dominion, being god, born of a god and a goddess, like Horus, the son of Isis and Osiris, who has avenged his father Osiris; towards the gods, full of generous piety, has consecrated to the temples revenues of money and provisions; and has supported great expenses in order to bring tranquillity to Egypt, and to establish order in all that concerns sacred affairs, has manifested with all his own power his sentiments of humanity; and of the public revenues and imposts collected in Egypt, he has finally suppressed some, and lightened others, so that the people and all the others may have plenty under his reign; the sums due to the treasury by the inhabitants of Egypt, and those of the rest of his kingdom, which were very

considerable, he has generally remitted ; and those imprisoned
and those against whom law suits had commenced long since,
he has freed them from all claims ; he has moreover ordered
that the revenues of the temples, and the contributions which
had been granted them yearly, whether in provision or money, as
also the proper portions assigned to the gods, as the vineyards,
gardens, and other lands, that belonged to the gods under the
reign of his father, should remain on the same footing.   As to
the priests, he has also commanded that they should pay nothing
more to the appointment fund than what they had been taxed
to the first year under his father ; he has further remitted to
those amongst the sacred body annual voyage to Alexandria ; he
has likewise ordered that there should be no longer levied the
contribution for the navy; of the byssus delivered in the temples
to the royal treasury he has remitted two-thirds ; and all that
had been previously neglected, he has re-established in proper
order, taking all care that which it had been customary to
perform for the gods should be executed as it ought to be ; at
the same time he has distributed justice to all like Hermes,
the twice great ; he has moreover ordered, that the returned
emigrants, both of the soldiers and all others who had shown
opposition in time of troubles, should keep the property in the
possession of which they had re-entered ; he has provided also
that of cavalry and infantry forces and ships should be sent
against those who had advanced against Egypt, whether by land
or sea, supporting great expenses in money and provisions, so
that the temples and all the inhabitants of Egypt should be in
safety.

Having gone to Lycopolis, which is in the Busirite nome, a
city which had been seized and fortified against a siege, by
great depôts of arms and every other kind of munitions, the

spirit of revolt having strengthened itself there for a long time, among the impious who are assembled in it, had done much mischief to the temples and inhabitants of Egypt ; and having laid siege to this place, he surrounded it with entrenchments, ditches, and strong walls. The Nile having made a great flood in the eighth year, and as it usually does, inundating the plains, the King has restrained it, in many places, by dyking the mouths of the rivers, for which works he has spent no small sum ; after having established both cavalry and infantry troops to watch them, he took in a short time the city by storm, and destroyed all the impious ones there, like Hermes and Horus, sons of Isis and Osiris, had mastered in these same localities the former revolters. As to the ringleaders of the rebels, under his father, and who had vexed the country without respecting the temples, he having come to Memphis to avenge his father and his own crown, he has punished them all as they deserved. At the time when he came to celebrate the ceremonies prescribed on receiving his crown, he further remitted from the temples that which was due to the royal treasury up to the eighth year, amounting in provisions and money to no small matter. Similarly he remitted the value of the cloth of the byssus which had not been furnished to the royal treasury, as also the expenses of verification for those which had been so, up to the same period. He has freed the temples from the tax of an *artabe* (about 10 gallons) per *aroura* (*i.e.*, the Egyptian acre) of sacred land; also of the *keramion* (*i.e.*, a measure) per *aroura* of vineyard. He made many donations to the Apis, to the Mnevis, and to the other sacred animals in Egypt, taking far more care than the Kings his predecessors of what relates to these animals in every circumstance ; and what was necessary to their burial he has given largely and nobly, as well as the

sums granted for their special worship, comprising therein the
sacrifice, panegyries, and other prescribed ceremonies. The
privileges of the temples of Egypt, he has maintained them on
the same footing, conformably to the laws ; he has embellished
the Apeion (*i.e.*, the abode of the Apis) with magnificent work,
having spent for this temple in gold, silver, and precious stones
a no small quantity. He has founded temples, shrines, and
altars ; he has restored in turn those that required repairs,
having for all that concerns the divinity, the zeal of a beneficent
god. After new information, he has repaired the chief
honoured temples under his reign as is fit. In reward of which,
the gods have given him health, victory, might, and all other
good things, the crown to remain with him and his children
for all time.

To Good Fortune.

It has seemed fit to the priests of all the temples in the
country, that all the honours bestowed to the ever-living King
Ptolemy, beloved of Ptah, the god Epiphanes, Eucharistes,
as well as those of his parents, gods Philopatores, and those of
his grand-parents, gods Euergetai, and those of the gods
Adelphi, and those of the gods Soteres, should be greatly
increased, and to raise to the ever-living King Ptolemy god
Epiphanes, Eucharistes, an image in each temple, in the
most visible part, which should bear the name of Ptolemy, the
avenger of Egypt ; that close by should be placed standing
the principal god of the temple, presenting him a weapon of
victory, the whole disposed in the Egyptian fashion ; that the
Priests should perform thrice daily religious services at the
images, and place sacred decorations on them ; and they should
execute the other prescribed ceremonies, as for the other gods,

in the panegyries celebrated in Egypt; that they should raise
to King Ptolemy, god Epiphanes, Eucharistes, born of the King
Ptolemy and the Queen Arsinoë, the gods Philopatores, a
statue of wood, and gilt shrine, in each of the temples; that
they should place them in the sanctuaries with the other shrines;
and that at the great panegyries when the shrines are taken
out, that of the god Epiphanes, Eucharistes, should be taken
out at the same time; in order that his shrine should be
distinguished from the others, now and hereafter, it should be
.surmounted with the ten gold diadems of the King, before
which should be placed an asp, as with all the diadems which
bear asps on the other shrines; that amidst them should be
placed the head-dress called Pschent, wherewith the King was
covered when he entered the temple at Memphis, there to
accomplish the ceremonies prescribed when taking possession
of the throne; that should be placed on the square face of the
head-dresses to the aforesaid royal ornament, ten golden
phylacteries, whereon shall be written that it is that of the King
who has rendered illustrious the Upper Country and the Lower
Country; and since the thirtieth of Mesori, when the King's
birthday is celebrated, as also the seventeenth of Mechir, when
he received the crown from his father (the Priests) have
recognized them as eponymous in the temples, which days are
really cause of many good things for all men : that they should
be celebrated in honour of him by a panegyry in the temples
of Egypt, monthly that they should perform in them sacrifices,
libations, and all other things appointed as in the other
panegyries, as well as the . . . . in the temples; that
they should celebrate a feast and a panegyry for the ever-living
and beloved of Ptah, King Ptolemy, god Epiphanes, Eucharistes
yearly in all the temples of the country, from the first of Thoth,

during five days, wherein they should also bear crowns, performing the sacrifices and libations and all that is proper ; that the Priests of the other gods should receive the names of Priests of the god Epiphanes, Eucharistes, besides the other names of the gods of whom they are the Priests ; and that they should mention, in all the decrees and declarations that be written by them, the priesthood of the King; that every individual may be permitted to celebrate the *fête*, to set up the aforesaid shrine, and to have it by him, accomplishing all the ceremonies prescribed in the festivals monthly and annually, so that it may be known that the Egyptians (increase) the honours, and honour the god Epiphanes, Eucharistes the King, as it is legal to do ; finally that this decree be engraved on a tablet of hard stone, in hieroglyphic, enchorial (or demotic), and Greek characters ; and place it in every temple of the first, second, and third class, near the image of the ever-living King.

After the Greek part of the inscription had been read, an attempt was made to unravel the enchorial or demotic part, for it was considered to be alphabetic ; but subsequent research proved that this view was wrong. The eminent French Oriental scholar Silvestre de Sacy also worked at the demotic, and succeeded in indicating the equivalents of the proper names in the Greek version. Later, Akerblad[1] the Swede gave himself up to the study of the same part of the inscription, and this scholar was so successful that he was enabled to find and fix the

---

[1] ' Lettre sur l'Inscription Égyptienne du Monument de Rosette,' 8vo. Paris, 1802.

value of some of the characters which formed the proper names ; though, curiously enough, but little was done towards the decipherment of the hieroglyphic part of the inscription. A study of the Greek and demotic parts of the inscription showed that the words Alexander and Alexandria in the fourth and seventeenth lines of the Greek inscriptions corresponded to two other groups in the second and tenth line of the demotic inscription ; that a group of characters, repeated about thirty times in the demotic or enchorial inscriptions, corresponded to the word 'king' in the Greek ; and that a group of characters, recurring fourteen times in the demotic or enchorial, corresponded to the word Ptolemy which occurs eleven times in the Greek, etc.[1]

All these little discoveries were helps towards the grand object of the decipherment of the Egyptian hieroglyphics ; but it seems very probable that this would have been accomplished much sooner had not the scholars of the day had their heads filled with ideas on the subject which not only led them astray, but which stopped the progress of the work ; though why they held their peculiar views, or from whence they obtained them, is hard to say. As an example of these, Dr. Birch says 'the Chevalier Palin, in 1802–4, did not hesitate to assert that it was only necessary to translate the Psalms of David into Chinese, and write them in the

---

[1] Dr. Birch, ' Introduction to the Study of Egyptian Hieroglyphs,' p. 194 : and see Young in the 'Encyclopædia Britannica :' London, 1828, art. Hieroglyphics.

ancient character of that language, in order to reproduce
the Egyptian papyri, and that these latter contained many
Biblical books.   In 1806 M. von Hammer had given to
the world the translation of the work of some Arabic
charlatan, which professed to explain the hieroglyphics.
Lenoir, in 1810, considered them to be Hebrew documents.   An anonymous author, in 1812, thought that
the inscription of the portico of Dendera contained a
translation into hieroglyphs of the Hundredth Psalm.'[1]

If possible, still more absurd statements on the subject
of the contents of Egyptian inscriptions were made : it
was gravely asserted that one text contained an account
of a battle between the wicked and the good in the early
days of the Egyptian empire about 4000 B.C. ; that
portions of the Bible would be found in another, and that
a third contained abstruse philosophical ideas.   It is sad
to see what an amount of learning and energy was
utterly wasted in the attempt to prove these absurd
theories.

But among all this chaos and confusion there were
two men quietly working at the decipherment of
Egyptian in different parts of Europe, and independently
of each other, viz., Thomas Young, born 1773, and
François Champollion, born at Grenoble in 1790.   It
was suggested to Young that the unknown language of
the Rosetta Stone was capable of being resolved into an
alphabet of thirty letters ;[2] and a very brief account of

---

[1] Dr. Birch, in Wilkinson's 'The Egyptians,' p. 194.
[2] By Prof. Vater, *ibid.*, p. 195.

his labours is as follows. He published some account of the demotic or enchorial writing in the 'Journal of the Society of Antiquaries' in 1817; he was not very successful in identifying the groups of hieroglyphs, though after a time he found out the name of Ptolemy, and that the first hieroglyph in the name was the equivalent of the demotic or enchorial form. He obtained this result by arguing that if the demotic was phonetic, the hieroglyphic must be also. He picked out from the inscriptions the cartouches of Ptolemy and Berenice; and in each of these he identified the phonetic value of some of the characters; but when he tried to read other names by these he failed; for example, he read Autocrator for Arsinoë, and Cæsar for Euergetes. His contribution to the decipherment amounted to the identification of five characters, and this is all that can be said. Much of his work, as Dr. Birch has said, is 'beneath criticism,' and he failed alike by attributing wrong values to some of the characters, and by his interpretation of the meaning of them. As a physicist, however, Thomas Young was a great thinker, and a very celebrated man: but it is not true that he deciphered the Egyptian hieroglyphics, or even that his labours assisted the real decipherer, Champollion; because he had studied and knew a great deal more about demotic rather than the hieroglyphic language.

About the year 1818, Champollion began the study of Egyptian. He had busied himself before this date in studying the Coptic language and the geography of

ancient Egypt ; and as he had read and studied all that
the ancients had written upon the subject of Egyptian,
he was exceedingly well prepared to grapple with the
difficult task before him.   The unfortunate Belzoni had
found at Philæ a small obelisk which had a Greek
inscription on the base, and one in hieroglyphics on
the shaft.   A copy of the Greek text was sent in 1822
to Letronne, and afterwards another containing the
hieroglyphs.   He at once considered that the latter
must contain the same matter as the former.   Here
Champollion's work began.   It was argued that the
subject matter of the Greek would be translated into
hieroglyphs, but as the Greek proper names would not
give any sense in Egyptian, they could not be translated :
therefore it is absolutely necessary that the *sounds* which
formed the proper names in Greek should be written in
Egyptian characters.   If this argument is correct, certain
phonetic signs or characters stand revealed.

In the Egyptian text of the obelisk we have a group of
signs enclosed in an oval, and this group is repeated a
large number of times.   Now the name of Ptolemy occurs
in the Greek several times, therefore this group of hieroglyphs must represent the name Ptolemy.   If this is
the case, then the first sign is P, the second T, and so on.
Now the way to prove if these signs have been rightly
read, is to apply them to other names written both in
hieroglyphs and in Greek where these same signs or
letters occur or are supposed to occur.   The Greek
inscription mentioned above gave the name of a king

called Ptolemy, and of a queen called Cleopatra ; on comparing the hieroglyphic signs which were supposed to be the equivalent of the Greek name Ptolemaios, with the group on the Rosetta Stone also supposed to be Ptolemaios, they were found to correspond exactly ; hence it was certain that the group was the Greek name Ptolemy written in hieroglyphic letters. If now the first name on the obelisk of Philæ was that of Ptolemy, the second must be that of Cleopatra.

The following is the way in which the names Ptolemy and Cleopatra are written in Egyptian characters :—

I. Cleopatra.

II. Ptolemy, living for ever, beloved of the god Ptah.

Next, Champollion supposed that each hieroglyph had the value of the initial syllable of the object which is represented,[1] and re-writing these names with numbers attached to each sign, we have :—

I. Cleopatra.

1.	2.	3.	4.	5.	6.	7.	8.	9.	10.	11.

[1] Dr. Birch, in Wilkinson's 'The Egyptians,' p. 199.

II. Ptolemy.

1. ☐ 2. ◠ 3. ⸘ 4. ⊜ 5. ⊂⊃ 6. ⟨ 7. ⟨ 8. ⟨ [1]

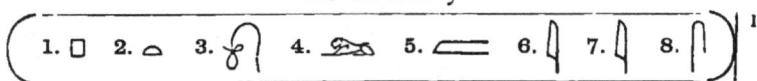

Now, sign No. 1 in the name Cleopatra represents a 'knee,' and as the Coptic[2] word for knee begins with *k*, this sign should be K.

Sign No. 2 in the same name represents a 'lion ;' as the Coptic word for lion begins with *l*, this sign should be L. It will be noticed that this same sign occurs in the name of Ptolemy, No. 4.

Sign No. 3 in the same name represents a 'reed,' and forms Nos. 6 and 7 in the name Ptolemy ; as the Coptic word for reed begins with *a*, this sign should be A or E.

Sign No. 4 in the same name represents a ' noose,' and must be equivalent to O. Sign No. 5 in the same name, being the same as No. 1 in the name Ptolemy, must therefore be P. Sign No. 6 in the same name represents an ' eagle ;' and as the Coptic word for eagle begins with *a*, and as it is the same as sign No. 9 in the name Cleopatra in the place where the *a* recurs, it must be A. Sign No. 7 represents a 'hand ;' as the Coptic name for hand begins with *t*, this sign should be T. Sign No. 8, in the same name, represents a ' mouth;' as the Coptic word for mouth begins with *r*, this sign should be R. Of sign No. 9 we have already spoken. Signs

---

[1] We omit here the other signs which are given in the cartouche above, as they form titles of the king, and are not necessary for our present purpose.

[2] The ancient Egyptian language is the mother of Coptic.

No. 10 (the same as No. 2 in the name Ptolemy) and No. 11 have no equivalent in the Greek ; but subsequent researches have proved that these signs are placed after the name of a female. If we look at the signs in the name of Ptolemaios, we find that only Nos. 5 and 8 remain without values, and it is easy to see from the Greek that they must represent M and S respectively.

Going back now to the signs ⬚ 𝍕 ⟩ in the unnumbered cartouche, we recognize the first two ▢ at once, for we have had them both in the names of Ptolemy and Cleopatra ; and as the Greek version tells us that Ptolemy is ' beloved of Phtha,' we know that the third sign 𝍕 must have the value *ḥ*, and that the fourth must mean ' beloved.' Champollion, after studying the other names of the later rulers of Egypt, was enabled to put together a very fair list of values of the signs, and by continuous work and study he succeeded in finding out many of the more difficult values of rare and uncommon signs. All difficulties were not yet overcome, for some of the signs were syllabic ; but little by little these difficulties melted away, and it became certain that the entire solution of the problem of Egyptian decipherment was not very far off.

For about nine years Champollion pursued his studies in the most unremitting manner, and work after work issued from his pen, containing texts, translations, explanations and information of the greatest value about ancient Egypt and its people.

But although Champollion had, quite alone, set the
decipherment of Egyptian upon a sure and firm base,
there lacked not men who started new theories on the
subject, and fought for them with a degree of fierceness
and zeal that now appear almost incredible.   A
large number of people objected to such a simple
explanation of the hieroglyphics, and wished and hoped .
to find in them something of the mysterious and the
marvellous.   Others maintained that the language was
sacred, and proceeded to divide the signs into classes,
to understand which is more difficult than Egyptian
itself.   Worse than all, there still appeared works
containing explanations of Egyptian texts based upon
the old ideographic theory;[1] and Klaproth attacked
Champollion on every possible occasion, relying upon
his having found out a few small and unimportant details
in which Champollion had tripped ; while others still
believed in the absurd interpretations published by
Kircher in his 'Œdipus Aegyptiacus.'   Little by little,
however, Champollion's system was gaining ground, and
many scholars who published works at that time
hastened to supplement their arguments by proofs drawn
from the new source of information.

About the year 1837 the late Dr. Lepsius published
a letter to Rosellini, in which he analysed and laid down
the structure of the language in his usual masterly

---

[1] For example, Janelli on the Rosetta Stone, published under the title of
' Fundamenta Hermeneutica Hieroglyphicæ Crypticæ veterum Gentium.'
8vo.   Neapol., 1830.

manner; and from this time onwards the good work advanced rapidly.   Students arose in England, France, Germany, Italy, and elsewhere ; but until very recently there remained some who persistently refused to acknowledge that Champollion's system of decipherment was the true one ; and so late as 1862 Sir G. C. Lewis maintained in his 'Astronomy of the Ancients' that, practically, the tradition of the Egyptian language had not been preserved unbroken, either in writing or orally, and since a period had elapsed during which it was entirely forgotten, it could never be restored.   For the refutation of this gentleman's ideas, the reader is referred to the learned and masterly article by Mr. Renouf in the 'Atlantis,' Vol. IV., 1861, pp. 23–57.

Thus has grown the edifice of the decipherment of the Egyptian hieroglyphics, the stones bearing them, some little, some big, having been shaped ages ago in many distant lands.   By reading two names on the obelisk of Philæ and on the Rosetta Stone, and by spelling out the Greek, Roman, and Persian names of the rulers of Egypt, has this great work been accomplished.

CHAPTER II.

The Egyptian Language and Writing.

The Egyptians used a variety of substances for writing upon, such as stone, wood, leather, linen, and papyrus. When stone of any sort was used for this purpose the characters were cut into it with a chisel : and many of the inscriptions upon sandstone and the like were filled in with the most beautiful colours. Unfortunately, however, much of the colour has disappeared and now, in many cases, only traces of it can be seen. In the better class of sculptures the details of the object represented are most carefully carved, and some characters are cut into the stone to the depth of nearly an inch. In the case of wood, the characters are sometimes cut as in stone, and sometimes merely painted.

Papyrus was the material which was in the greatest demand for making copies of the Book of the Dead, literary compositions, and official documents. The plant grew in Upper Egypt, the Delta, and other parts of the country. To fit it for writing purposes the interior of the stalks were cut into thin slices in the direction of their length ; these were laid on a board in a row, and similar slices were placed upon them at

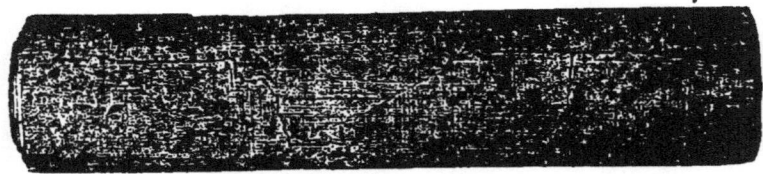

Roll of papyrus in the British Museum.

Wooden palette with reeds for writing which belonged originally to "Amâsis the good god, and lord of the two countries," British Museum.

right angles ; and when their surfaces had been joined by a kind of gum or glue, and pressed and dried, the papyrus was complete.[1] Inscribed papyri are of different widths, viz., six, eleven, twelve and a half, thirteen and even fourteen and a half inches ; while their length varies from a few inches to one hundred and fifty feet.[2]

The scribe wrote on papyrus with a reed, the hieroglyphs being generally traced in outline. He carried his inks in small hollows in his palette. The greater part of the ordinary inscriptions on papyrus are written with black ink, but directions for the repetition of certain passages or rubrics, and the initial paragraphs, are written with red. Texts written in other colours are found, but they are not common. Where it was possible the scribe represented an object in its natural colour ; he made the sun red, the moon yellow, trees, plants, and all vegetables, green ; but objects requiring out of the way colours were not so well done, owing to the comparatively limited supply of colours at the disposal of the scribe. Reeds cut like modern pens were also used for writing, and specimens of these may be seen in the British Museum (North Gallery, 2nd Egyptian Room).

The scribe's palettes were made of wood, ivory, and stone ; they were of different lengths and widths, varying from five or six inches to twenty in length, and from two to three inches in breadth. They were frequently

---

[1] Wilkinson's ‘Ancient Egyptians,’ ii. p. 180.

[2] Dr. Birch, in Wilkinson's ‘Ancient Egyptians,’ ii. p. 182 ; Bunsen's ‘Egypt,’ v. p. 590.

inscribed, and at times the characters were most beautifully inlaid with lapis lazuli. There is an oblong hollow in them wherein the writing reeds may be placed ; and at the end are generally shallow holes for the ink, traces of which, of a red and black colour, still remain in some of them. Palettes are sometimes dedicated to the god Thoth, and the British Museum possesses among others one which originally belonged to a scribe of the time of Amenophis III. (about B.C. 1500), and one of a scribe who lived in the time of Rameses II. (about B.C. 1350). In this latter, five of the scribe's reeds still remain. The office of scribe was very important, and was generally held by a person belonging to the priestly or first caste of Egyptians.[1]

The hierogylphics may be divided into two classes : (1) those representing ideas, and (2) those used for sounds. For example, the picture of an obelisk, ⎰, expressed that object ; 🦅, a vulture, expressed that bird ; and so on. Sometimes, however, the cause was put for the effect, and the reverse : thus 🖋 a palette and reed, represented 'writing' (also 'scribe') ; and 𓎛, dishevelled hair, stood for 'grieving,' because the hair was disturbed and uncared for in a time of trouble. It will be readily understood that the ideographic part of the writing is much older than the phonetic ; and in the very early texts we find the use of ideographs greater than in those of a later period.

---

[1] Wilkinson's 'Ancient Egyptians,' i. p. 157.

This is what one would expect, because all nations use a pictorial language long before they come to phonetics.

The pictorial method of representation in the texts is exceedingly useful, for it frequently suggests the right meaning of a word ; and where new words are found phonetically spelt, but without ideographs, it is often difficult to find out what they mean. An ideograph was often repeated three or more times, to express the plural, thus :—⯒ ⯒ ⯒ 'bones,' ⯒ 'doors,' ⯒ ⯒ ⯒ 'gods,' ⯒ ⯒ ⯒ 'glorified souls,' ⯒ ⯒ ⯒ 'seats,' ⯒ ⯒ ⯒ 'roads,' and ⯒⯒⯒⯒⯒⯒⯒⯒⯒⯒⯒⯒⯒⯒⯒⯒ 'the two cycles of the gods.' It must be mentioned that every hieroglyph could be used to express the sound of the object which it represented.[1] Custom, however, set aside a certain number which were used to express the sounds of other objects. For example ⯒ represents a 'plough,' and ⯒ a 'mouth,' but ⯒ means 'beloved ;' ⯒ represents a 'mouth,' and ⯒ 'water'; but ⯒ means 'name.'

Under the class of phonetics must also be mentioned those which have syllabic values, such as ⯒ *mer*, ⯒ *ḥem*, and ⯒ *neb*. A large number of these are used as determinative of sound : for example, the value of ⯒ is *ānχ*, but we find ⯒ ⯒, *i.e.*, *ā-n-χ* + the syllable ⯒ ;also ⯒ ⯒ *i.e.*, *ā-n* + the syllable ⯒, and so on.

[1] Dr. Birch, in Bunsen's ' Egypt,' v. p. 597.

Certain hieroglyphs were used as *Determinatives.*
By a Determinative is meant a sign which represents
the *idea*, either directly or indirectly, of the word written ;
and a determinative could be placed either before or
after a word. For example, in the word for 'child,'
χ*rot*, the first three signs give the word for
child, and then follows the determinative, which is the
picture of a child; the word *āpš*, means
'tortoise ;' but it is written in the texts with the
picture for 'tortoise' after it ; so, . The few
following words will illustrate the way in which the
phonetic signs and ideographs are employed in writing
words :—

sesh	...	bird's nest.
iart	...	scorpion.
mau	...	cat.
menfat	...	soldier.
qerḥu	...	night.
ubn	...	to shine.
āua	...	ox.
emsuḥ	...	crocodile.
ḥfi	...	worm.

(hieroglyphs)	*māχait*	...	pair of scales.
(hieroglyphs)	*āf*	...	bee.
(hieroglyphs)	*àāḥ*	...	moon.
(hieroglyphs)	*àāāni*	...	ape.
(hieroglyphs)	*neràu*	...	vulture.

The number of hieroglyphic signs may be considered to be about two thousand, and a short list of the commoner phonetics is as follows :—

(hieroglyph)	*a*	(hieroglyph)	*i*	(hieroglyph)	*s*
(hieroglyph)	*à*	(hieroglyph)	*k*	(hieroglyph)	*š* (or *sh*)
(hieroglyph)	*ā*	(hieroglyph)	*ḳ*	(hieroglyph)	*t*
(hieroglyph)	*b*	(hieroglyph)	*l*	(hieroglyph)	*th*
(hieroglyph)	*p*	(hieroglyph)	*m*	(hieroglyph)	*ṭ*
(hieroglyph)	*f*	(hieroglyph)	*n*	(hieroglyph)	*ṭ*
(hieroglyph)	*h*	(hieroglyph)	*q*	(hieroglyph)	*u*
(hieroglyph)	*ḥ* (or *kh*)	(hieroglyph)	*r*	(hieroglyph)	*χ*

The arrangement of the hieroglyphics in inscriptions varies, but generally they face to the right, and are read from right to left like Arabic, Syriac, Hebrew, etc. Sometimes they face to the left, and are to be read from left to right; but very often they are arranged in perpendicular rows, with carefully drawn lines separating

each row.   Instances have occurred where the characters
face in one direction, but are to be read in the other.

The hieroglyphics were particularly useful for the
purpose of ornament ; and when each hieroglyphic is
painted in the colours which most nearly resembles the
object which it represents, the effect is vivid and
gorgeous.   The scribe or mason frequently sacrificed
the strict order of the letters in a word to his love of
symmetrical arrangement : in the papyri, however, the
right order is usually kept.   For an example of the
ornamental effect produced by a collection of hieroglyphs,
see the extract from the text inscribed upon the Pyramid
of Pepi, printed round pages 110, 111 : and the following
is a specimen of Egyptian with interlinear transliteration,
and literal translation.

SPECIMEN OF INTERLINEAR TRANSLITERATION
AND TRANSLATION.[1]

au   arna   hesest   ret   hercret   nutaru heres
Done have I behests of men and the will of the gods ;

au   ta - na   ta   en   heqr   sesau - na
wherefore given have I bread to the hungry, satiated have I

atet   au   ses - na   nutar   em   pa - f   an
the indigent, followed have I the god in house his, not

[1] See 'Trans. Soc. Bib. Arch.,' vol. viii. p. 309.

āa   re - à   em   śenit   àn
hath magnified mouth my against superior officers, not is

peṭ   em   nemt - à   śem - à   ḥer sa   χenṭ
there stretch in stride my, walk I according to measure.

àr - nà   em   māt   mer   en   suten
Done have I   law   beloved by the king,

13.   reχ - kuà   entet   utu - nef   set   res - nà
knew I   what   commanded he it,   watched I

ḥer àst - à   er   seqa   baiu - f   ṭūa - na   ṭua - f
at seat my   to   exalt will his, rose I for worship his

hru   neb   er ṭa - nà   àb - à   χenti   14.   t'eṭ - f
day every,   gave I   heart my to what   said he

àn   māhi   ḥer   śa - nef   χer - à
without hesitating at what determined he { *with reference*
                                            to me, }

ṭet - ná	metrit (?)	ḥnā	metit
took I	*uprightness*	*and*	*fairness,*

peḥ - ná   enen   her kar - á   qebeb   ḥesna - uá
arrived I at what was for silence, refreshing, favoured me

neb - á   her   menχ - á   maa - nef   rut
lord the king my for beneficence my, saw he that vigorous

āā - á   án   áb - á   seχenti   ást - á
were hands my through heart my advancing seat my.

Hieroglyphics were employed for inscriptions on public monuments, etc., but two other characters of writing are found, the hieratic, and the demotic or enchorial; this latter is not comparatively very ancient, and a specimen of it is given in the reproduction of the Rosetta Stone p. 20. The hieratic was the *cursive* hand, and was much used by the priests in making their reports of government transactions, and in writing down literary compositions. It was taken from the hieroglyphic, as the following example, with the hieroglyphic transcription beneath, will show.

Hieratic Writing.[1]

TRANSCRIPTION.

To what group or family of languages Egyptian belongs, is at present an undecided point: there is a great influx of Semitic words about 1400 B.C.; for further information on this subject the reader is referred to the works of Benfey, Lepsius, Brugsch, Renan, and others.

[1] See Birch, 'Select Papyri in the Hieratic Character,' Part II, pl. xi, page 5, line 9, and page 6, line 1. The hieratic text is written from right to left, but the hieroglyphs read the opposite way.

CHAPTER III.

THE LAND OF EGYPT, ITS PEOPLE AND THEIR HISTORY.

EGYPT lies between the twenty-fourth and thirty-second
parallels of north latitude, in the north-east of Africa ;
it is about six hundred miles long, and is really com-
prised of a strip of land on each bank of the Nile.
This strip varies in width from ten to thirty miles.
The Egyptians called their country Kem, *i.e.*, ' the
black,' because of the very dark colour of the soil.   It
bore a variety of names, each having some particular
application ; and among these must come Ta-mera,
which means the ' land of the inundation.'   The
Assyrians called the land *Musur*, the Hebrews *Misraim*,
and the Arabs to this day *Misr*.   The Egyptian kings
called themselves 'lords of the two countries,' thereby
indicating that the land was divided into two great
parts, the north and the south : very probably a
remembrance of the ' double ' land is preserved in the
Hebrew name *Misraim*, which is a dual form.   The
kings are also called on the monuments ' lords of the
white and red crown ;' the former signifying their rule
over Upper Egypt, and the latter their dominion over

Lower Egypt. Upper Egypt was divided into twenty-two nomes, and Lower Egypt into twenty.[1] Hitherto the name 'Egypt' has remained unexplained; but some have supposed that it is derived from Ḥa-ka-ptaḥ, (i.e., the temple of the genius of Ptah), the sacred name of Memphis.

From what country did the Egyptians come? Ethnologists and anthropologists, having examined a large number of skulls of mummies, have come to the conclusion that the Egyptians belong to the Caucasian race. Hence it is generally understood now that some thousands of years before the Christian era (how many it is quite impossible to say) the nation which afterwards inhabited the Nile set out from Asia, for some reason still unexplained, journeyed westward, and crossing the Isthmus of Suez, entered Africa, and settling down by the Nile, founded there a mighty kingdom. This agrees too with what is stated in the table of nations given by Moses, who says, 'And the sons of Ham; Cush, and Mizraim, and Phut, and Canaan.'[2] Now Ham (or Kham) is the same as Khem, Egypt, and a proof of this may be deduced from the Psalms, where it is said, 'And smote all the firstborn in Egypt; the chief of their strength in the tabernacles of Ham;'[3] and again, 'Wondrous works in the land of Ham, and terrible things by the Red Sea.'[4] Now the Mizraim mentioned in the table of nations is Egypt itself.

---

[1] For a list, see Brugsch, 'Egypt under the Pharaohs,' ii. p. 8.
[2] Gen. x. 6.   [3] Ps. lxxviii. 51.   [4] Ps. cvi. 22.

As for the other sons of Ham, the inhabitants of
Kush, *i.e.*, the region called after the son of Ham, are
represented on the Egyptian monuments. Their bodily
appearance is the same, though their skin is a little
darker, and at the outset they appear to have had a
religion and speech akin to that of the Egyptians.[1] We
find Phut, most probably, in the Punt of the inscriptions,
the land from whence spices came, which was situated
to the south of Egypt on both sides of the Red Sea. As
early as 2500 years before Christ, the hieroglyphics tell us
that a king of Egypt sent one of his people called Anti,
to bring back a peculiarly valuable kind of frankincense
from this land. The fourth son, Canaan, is represented
by the original inhabitants of Canaan, who were probably near relatives of the Egyptians. It has been
thought by some scholars that there are indications in
the inscriptions which would lead one to suppose that
the Egyptians considered that the home of the race was
the Nile ; this idea, however, has never been worked out.
Some again, following a Greek tradition, have thought
that the civilization of Egypt came from Ethiopia ; but
all modern researches show that this idea has no ground-
work of truth.

The Egyptians of the later empire believed that men
had been made out of clay upon a potter's wheel·
They believed that the god Harmachis[2] attacked his foes,
who fled in all directions from before him. Those who

---

[1] Wiedemann, 'Ægyptische Geschichte,' p. 23.
[2] Chabas, 'Etudes,' p. 1 ; Naville, 'Mythe d'Horus.'

came to the south became the Cushites, those who came
to the north became the Amu, those who came to the
west the Libyans, and those who came to the east the
Shasu; and thus were the four races of mankind made.
Of the Amu more will be said further on; for it was
from this race that the Khita nation, so celebrated for
having waged war successfully with Rameses II., and
recently identified with the Biblical Hittites, sprang.

What was the Egyptian like in stature? His head was
large, his forehead square, his eyes large, his cheeks full,
his mouth wide, his nose short and rounded, and his lips
thick.[1]

The ancient history of Egypt goes back into a far distant past. The exact time when the early settlers on the
Nile first made their home in the ' black ' land is quite
unknown; and who ruled them and gave them laws is,
historically, also unknown. Only one thing about the
matter is quite certain, and that is that the migration
from the East must have taken place some thousands of
years before Christ.

The Egyptians believed that the first three dynasties
of kings who ruled over Egypt were composed of gods,
who reigned in succession, and of a series of beings who
were called ' the followers of Horus.'[2]

The first dynasty consisted of a number of gods,
Ptah, Rā, Shu, Seb, Osiris, Set or Typhon, and Horus:
these were supposed to have reigned for 12,300 years,

[1] Wiedemann, ' Ægyptische Geschichte,' p. 25.
[2] Maspero, ' Histoire Ancienne, p. 18.

according to Manetho, a celebrated priest of Heliopolis who flourished about B. C. 261. Of the next two dynasties we only know that they were termed, it is supposed, 'the followers of Horus.' So that at present nothing is really known of the Egyptian rulers before Menes, the first historical king of Egypt. Many dates · have been fixed by scholars for the reign of this king: Champollion-Figeac thought about B.C. 5867, Bunsen 3623, Lepsius 3892, Brugsch 4455, and Wilkinson 2320; but it must be understood that a correct chronology of the early empire of Egypt is not at present possible, for only *approximate* data can be given.[1]

Mena or Menes, the first king of Egypt, came from the town of Teni, the Greek This, near Abydos. According to Herodotus, he built the great temple of Ptah, established a regular worship there, and is said to have founded the great city of Memphis, which name means 'the good place.' He built a large dyke to protect this city, and it is that which even to-day protects Gizeh from excessive inundation. He was a mighty warrior, and waged war with the Libyans. The tradition of his death is that he was devoured by a

---

[1] Since it is impossible to give here an account of each king of Egypt and his works, we can only refer to the most important of them, reserving our special attention for those kings with whom the children of Israel came in contact. On pages 12 to 14 we have given a list of the kings and the approximate dates of their reigns from Brugsch's ' Egypt under the Pharaohs :' and for fuller information on matters of Egyptian history we refer the reader to Dr. Birch's ' Egypt,' Wiedemann's ' Ægyptische Geschichte,' and the above-mentioned work of Brugsch.

crocodile.   He was succeeded by his son Athothis, who
is said to have written books on anatomy.   Remarkably
little is known of Menes, for none of his inscriptions
have been found ; his name, however, is placed first in
the list of kings.

The next Egyptian king of importance was Áta, or as
the Greeks called him, Ouenephes ; and he is famous for
having built pyramids at Kochome near Sakkarah.   Of
the remaining kings of the first and second dynasties but
little is known.   During the reign of Necherophes or
Nefer-ka-Seker, the first king of the third or Memphitic
dynasty, we are told by Manetho that an eclipse took
place, and the Libyans, with whom this king was
fighting, were so terrified that they submitted immediately.

The fourth dynasty was also from Memphis, and it was
under these kings that Egypt became famous ; it must
be remembered that at this period we are able to obtain
information from the monuments which the kings of the
fourth dynasty erected.   During the reign of Senefru

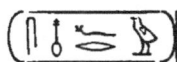 its first king, a very valuable mine of

turquoise was found in Arabia at Wady Magharah, and
traces of the workings, etc., are still to be seen.   An
invasion of the Amu took place in the reign of this king,
who appears to have been occupied in various wars.
Some have thought that the pyramid of Meydoum
marks the place of his sepulchre, but his body has not
hitherto been found.

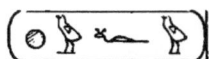

χufu, or Cheops (B.C. 3733), the successor of Senefru, is celebrated chiefly for the immense pyramid, called 'Height,' which he built at Gizeh, the height of which is 450 feet, and the breadth at the base 746 feet. The pyramids which come next in point of size are the pyramids of Chephren and Mycerinus; the former is 447 feet high, and measures 690 feet at the base; while the latter is 203 feet high, and measures 352 feet at the base. The pyramids were graves; the plan of construction, as laid down by Lepsius, is as follows: When a new king ascended the throne he began at once to build a pyramid. The site having been chosen, the ground was levelled, and a slanting shaft was bored out of the solid rock; and at the end of this shaft a rectangular chamber was made, which was intended to hold the sarcophagus containing the king's body. On the flat site a comparatively small building was made, the outsides of which were steep steps. If the king died at this stage of the work, he was laid in his sarcophagus, and the steep steps of the little building were filled up with triangular pieces of stone, and so its sides became smooth, and the pyramid, though little, was complete. If, on the other hand, the king lived another year, a second layer of stones was built on to the four sides of the pyramid; and for every year the king lived a fresh layer of stones was built on to the four sides; but the layers became gradually smaller. When the king died no further layers were added, and the pyramid was finished either by the steps being filled up with exactly fitting pieces of stone, or another layer of stones was added, and then the edges of the stones were chiselled away until each side of the structure was perfectly smooth. It is perfectly evident that such a tomb might well be considered everlasting, for it was inaccessible to the attacks of the elements, and its destruction would be a very difficult piece of work even for modern nations. The size of a pyramid then, varied generally with the length of the king's life ; but vanity and a desire to possess the largest pyramid, may have induced a king to add two layers or even more for each year of his life.

There are some who doubt the truth of this theory of pyramid construction, but it has been pointed out that the nearer the inside the better is the work found to be ; while each subsequent layer seems to have been more carelessly and hastily built than its fellow.[1] The Egyptian word for pyramid is *abmer*. The greater part of a pyramid was built of limestone, but red granite was used for certain parts, such as the interior of the passages, of the Great Pyramid. Small passages leading upwards and downwards are found inside some of the pyramids. When the mummy of the king had been deposited in the sarcophagus inside the chamber within the pyramid, all the various pathways were filled up with blocks of stone.

---

[1] Various elaborate theories have been propounded in respect of the building of the pyramids, and the reader is referred to Prof. Piazzi Smyth's works, and ' The Pyramids and Temples of Gizeh,' by Mr. W. M. F. Petrie.

Even to the Egyptians, who were accustomed to build pyramids, such constructions must have appeared difficult ; and an idea will be obtained of the amount of labour necessary for the building of the pyramid of Cheops, when we consider that the causeway along which the stone was brought took ten years to build, the work being performed by a gang of one hundred thousand men, changed every three months ; thus four million men were employed on this work alone, while it required seven millions more to build the pyramid itself.[1]

The number of chambers in the pyramids has been accounted for by supposing that when the pyramid was begun a subterranean chamber was made for the royal tomb : but when the king lived long, and the pyramid grew larger, they built another chamber and left the first one empty. If the king should still continue to live, and the pyramid grew very large, another chamber was built to receive his sarcophagus and mummy. These first chambers were then probably used for his queen or his relatives.

The family of Cheops was buried near his pyramid, and Lepsius, during his journey across the plains stretching from Meydoum to Memphis, found the remains of no less than seventy-five pyramids, including those of various members of the family of Cheops. Cheops waged war against his enemies, and the rocks in the Wady Maghara represent him not only in combat with them, but victorious over them. He is said to have been

---

[1] Birch, ' Egypt,' p. 35.

The Sphinx.

a great tyrant and a very wicked man; but Manetho
went so far as to say that in his old age he repented of
his folly and wrote a book, which posterity considered
holy.   Another story is that the Egyptian nation hated
him so bitterly on account of the forced labour which he
imposed upon them, that it was necessary to bury him in
a subterranean chamber surrounded on all sides by the
waters of the Nile.   During the reign of Cheops a
medical papyrus, now in the British Museum, was found
by a priest in a temple, by moonlight.[1]

$\chi\bar{a}f$-$R\bar{a}$ or Chephren, the successor of
Cheops, also built a pyramid, which he called ' Great,' near
that of Cheops ; it is most beautifully made, but is not so
large as that of his predecessor.   Chephren is also justly
renowned for having built the small temple behind the
Sphinx.   The Sphinx (called in Egyptian Ḥu) is really
an immense lion with a man's head and represented the
god Harmachis, or the sun on the horizon.   Between
its paws is a narrow way leading to a temple which has
been made in front of the figure ; and as the name of
Chephren is found in inscriptions on the spot, it has
been supposed by some that this king caused the Sphinx
to be hewn out of the living rock ; but it is not certain.
The total height of the monument is about 65 feet, and
its length about 190 feet.   The face of this magnificent
monster was originally coloured red, and covered with
polished stone, but almost every trace of this covering

[1] See ' Zeitschrift für Aegyptische Sprache,' 1871, p. 62.

has now disappeared. The beard is in the British Museum.
The features are said to have been solemn, majestic,
and benignant. Its nose has been quite destroyed, and
many visitors to the Sphinx now-a-days think that this
magnificent figure, which has seen hundreds of generations rise and decay, which has gazed across the fiery
sands of the desert for thousands of years, and to whom
the duration of an empire is but a few years, exists solely
for them to chip and carve their names upon.

Menkau-Rā, or Mycerinus, like his
two predecessors, built for himself a pyramid, and is
supposed to have reigned sixty-three years. Tradition
makes him to have been a pious and good king, and one
who was a devout worshipper of the god Osiris. An
attempt was made in the year 1196 A.D. to entirely
destroy the pyramid which he built; but in reality,
his pyramid, which is the third at Gizeh, is the least
damaged. Colonel Vyse says that when he had
reached the sarcophagus chamber inside the pyramid,
he found there the stone sarcophagus of the king, and
the wooden cover of the inside coffin, which was made
of cedar. The body of the king had been carried
to the upper chamber in the pyramid, and had
literally been torn to pieces, most probably when the
pyramid was broken open A.D. 1196 in search of treasure.
The sarcophagus and cover of the coffin were shipped on
board an English vessel; but, alas! the ship was wrecked
and the sarcophagus found a resting-place at the bottom

of the sea near Gibraltar. Fortunately the wooden cover
was cast up by the sea, and the British Museum (third
Egyptian Room) possesses this, together with a small
fragment of the stone sarcophagus, and some fragments
of the mummy. On the cover are two lines of inscription, which are translated by Dr. Birch:[1] 'Osiris, king of
Upper and Lower Egypt, Menkaura, the ever living, born
of Nut (the goddess of the celestial waters), substance of
Seb ; thy mother Nut is spread over thee ; she renders
thee divine by annihilating thy enemies. O king
Menkaura, living for ever.' These fragments of mummy,
coffin, and sarcophagus are of the greatest interest ; for
not only do they show that mummifying was at that
time a well-understood art, but they speak to us across
a gulf of five thousand five hundred years, and tell us
something of their religious views and ideas. Moreover,
there is very little difference between the shape of
the hieroglyphs of those days and those of a much later
date ; and however far we go back, we never come to
an inscription belonging to a period in which we can see
that the Egyptians were learning to write.

Mycerinus was followed by a king called Sheps-es-kaf,
and with him the great and important fourth dynasty
closes.

We pass over the kings of the fifth and sixth dynasties,
merely remarking that their united reigns occupied a
period of about four hundred years, and that what is

---

[1] For other versions, see Brugsch, ' Egypt under the Pharaohs,' p. 83 ; and
Wiedemann, ' Geschichte,' p. 192.

generally known as the 'Old Empire' came to an end
with this dynasty about three thousand years before
Christ.

Very little beyond the names of the kings who belonged
to the sixth, seventh, eighth, ninth, tenth, and eleventh
dynasties is known; and a gap of about five hundred
years occurs in the history which it is absolutely impossible to fill up in detail.

The first king of the twelfth dynasty was called
Amenemḥā; he did battle with a Lybian tribe called
the Mat'iu, and defeated the Uaua of Nubia in the twenty-
ninth year of his reign.   During his reign Egypt enjoyed
great tranquillity, and the people from the highest to the
lowest received the proper care due to them.   In his
later years a conspiracy was formed against him; but he
was fortunate enough to escape the death by which he
was threatened at the hand of his foes, who attacked
him in his bed-room at night.   His son Usertsen I. was
associated with him in the kingdom during the last
years of his reign; and he wrote a book for this son full
of instructive sayings, a late copy of which is now in the
British Museum.

Usertsen I. was occupied for some years in fighting a
confederacy of Ethiopian tribes; and during the first
years of his reign he built some magnificent edifices in
Heliopolis, and completed several of the works undertaken by his father; he also had gold brought from
Nubia, and turquoise from the peninsula of Sinai.   A
beautiful inscription at Beni-Hassan records that a

prince named Amen, at the head of four hundred men, accompanied the king in one of his Ethiopian wars ; he describes himself as being an upright, honest, and indefatigable servant of the king, doing his behests in and out of season ; rendering up to him whatever was due to him without keeping back the least particle for himself, giving strict justice to all, showing kindness to the fatherless and widow, the poor and the distressed, taking nought of the poor man's crop, nor accepting the person of a great man before his humbler fellow ; and he boasts that having ploughed the whole of his land from the north to the south, there was not a hungry person in the whole land. Following the example of his father, Usertsen I. associated his son Amenemhā II. in the rule of the kingdom during the last few years of his life, and the like was done by Amenemhā in respect of his son Usertsen II.   During the reign of this monarch there lived a prince called Khnum-hetep, the son of Nehara and his wife Bakat. His official position was that of chief of the district of Menat-Khufu, but our attention is drawn to him by his tomb, which still exists.

Everything connected with the life of an Egyptian, the appliances of art, the tools of trade, sacrificial scenes, and scenes of life itself, are represented by picture and hieroglyph on Egyptian tombs with wonderful accuracy and beauty. One scene more than all others demands our attention, for in it some have seen a representation of Jacob's arrival in Egypt. It would appear that a family of thirty-seven people belonging to the Āmu

E

race emigrated to Egypt in the reign of Usertsen II., and brought with them an eye-paint called *mestem*, which was considered of great value. The features of these people are Jewish, their garments are of different shape, pattern and colours from those of the Egyptians ; the leader is better dressed than his fellows, and is called Abesha. The rest of the company is composed of men (armed with bows and arrows, and spears), women, and children ; one man plays a seven-stringed lyre ; and then follow the baggage animals. At all events such a picture will give an idea of what the arrival of a party of foreigners in Egypt would look like ; and when we read in the hieroglyphs that the chief of the party brought the valuable eye unguent to the chief of the land, we are reminded of Jacob's speech to his sons, ' Carry down the man a present, a little balm, and a little honey, spices, and myrrh, nuts, and almonds.'[1]

The next king, Usertsen III., continued the wars against the Ethiopians, and built the fortress of Samneh. The struggle between the Ethiopians and the Egyptians appears to have been very severe ; and at Samneh there was a tablet erected which forbade any negroes to pass by this place, unless they were in boats laden with goats, oxen, or other animals. Eventually the Egyptians were victorious. About fifteen hundred years after, Thothmes II. deified king Usertsen III., and caused festivals to be celebrated in his honour.

Amenemḥā III., the successor of Usertsen III., is

[1] Gen. xliii. 11. (See Frontispiece also.)

renowned not for wars or conquests, but for a thoroughly useful piece of work, whose benefit to the people of that day it would be hard to estimate, and still harder to over-rate. It is well known that the prosperity of Egypt depends upon a regular inundation, neither too great nor too little, of the Nile. If it is too little, then there ensues a famine, and if it is too great, there is also a famine. Amenemhā III. sought to lessen the danger of the starvation of his people by building the enormous lake Moeris (in Egyptian *Mi-ur*, 'the great water'), in the district called the Fayoum, in the west of Egypt, in which the surplus water of the inundation might be stored up for use in time of need. It was surrounded on all sides by dams, and was connected by a canal with the Nile. The lake was stocked with fish. In the Museum at Boulak there is preserved part of a papyrus which gives a plan of the lake and canal. The constructor of this work also built a pyramid 246 feet high, and the wonderful palace called the Labyrinth, which some say had three hundred rooms above ground, and the same number below ; Herodotus, however, gives the immense number of four thousand five hundred.

The last king of the twelfth dynasty was Amenemhā IV. ; and from this period (about 2200 B.C.) to the eighteenth dynasty there is a gap of about five hundred years. It is during this break that the rule of the Hyksos or 'Shepherd Kings' comes in. Having migrated into Egypt from the East, they established themselves at Memphis, and made themselves masters of the whole country; but they were expelled from Egypt finally by Aḥmes, the first king of the eighteenth dynasty, about 1700 B.C. Before their downfall wars had been going on for several years between these rulers from the East and such of the native chiefs as were able to muster armed men and to make an attempt to liberate their country.

The British Museum possesses a very valuable papyrus relating to this period, the importance of which was first recognized by De Rougé. It appears that the last 'Shepherd King,' Āpepi II., was a worshipper of the god Sutech, and wishing to build a magnificent temple to this god, he sent and demanded assistance in the shape of men and materials for his work from the Egyptian prince called Sekenen Rā. The prince called a council, and determined to refuse to comply with this demand; but although Sekenen Rā began the rebellion against the usurpers of the throne of Egypt, he appears never to have attained the throne himself, for the next monarch of all Egypt was called Aḥmes, i.e., 'the child of the Moon,' who was descended from the kings of the seventeenth dynasty; the official position which he held under Sekenen Rā was 'chief of the sailors' in a vessel called the 'Calf.' He distinguished himself by his valour in a number of victorious battles at Avaris and the fortress of Sharuhen, by which the power of the 'Shepherd Kings' was utterly broken; and at length, having reconquered the land of Egypt, this mighty soldier took up the reins of government and became

king.   Under his firm but mild rule the temples, which
had been sadly neglected, were repaired, a temple
dedicated to Ptah at Memphis, and another to Amen-
Rā at Thebes.

Ȧhmes reigned twenty-two years, and married Ȧhmes-
Nefertari, a negress, who appears to have ruled for some
time after her husband's death.   Their son Amenhotep
ruled eleven years.   Following this monarch came
Thothmes I., who made expeditions into Mesopotamia,
attacked the Syrians, and among other buildings erected
two granite obelisks before the temple of Amen-Rā at
Thebes.   He was succeeded by his daughter, queen
Hatasu, who in compliance with public opinion
associated her brother Thothmes II. with her in the
kingdom.   Thothmes II. ruled apparently for a short time
only, and it is hard to say whether he was murdered,
or whether he died in peace.   After his death the queen
became sole ruler, put on the dress of a man, and gave
orders to have the name of her brother Thothmes II.
erased from the monuments.   During her reign an
expedition was undertaken to the land of Punt, or the
spice country ; and spices, gold, ivory, precious stones,
and all other products of this wonderful—and to the
Egyptians new—land were brought home.   Some trees
were brought home so large that it took six men to
carry each of them.   This queen also ordered two
magnificent monolith granite obelisks with shining
metal tops to be made, which should stand before
the gate of Thothmes I., and record her works for ever.

Later on in her reign she associated another brother, Thothmes III., with herself in the kingdom, but the same fate befell her as befell her brother Thothmes II. ; for wherever on the monuments she appears co-regent with Thothmes III., her name has been carefully chiselled out and destroyed.

Bust of Thothmes III.

After the death of Hatasu, ⟨⊙ ▭ 🪲⟩ Thothmes III. became sole ruler of Egypt. By his success in mighty wars, and by the enormous quantity of tribute with which he enriched the Egyptian nation, as well as by his numerous and beautiful buildings in Thebes, Memphis,

and Heliopolis, he deserves in all respects the name of
'great' among the Egyptian kings.   He marched into
Mesopotamia as far as Nineveh, and wherever he went
the nations hastened to submit to him, and to pay
tribute; the few that would not do this, but preferred
to do battle with him, were ignominiously defeated.
Ethiopia, Syria, and Phœnicia were among the principal
countries that paid immense tribute ; and the record of
the wars of this monarch, and the enumeration of the
different amounts of tribute received, are sufficient to form
a large decoration for the sandstone wall which surrounds
the temple at Thebes, which he built.   Among the lists
of the peoples conquered by Thothmes III. occurs the
name *Aperu*, which some have considered to represent
the Hebrews.   The reader will be familiar with the name
of Thothmes III., for it was this king who had made,
and inscribed with his own name, the obelisk which is
commonly known as 'Cleopatra's Needle,' which now
stands on the Thames Embankment.[1]   Thothmes reigned
fifty-four years, and was succeeded by Amenhotep II.,
who after a short reign made way for Thothmes IV., the
king mentioned on the tablet between the forepaws of
the Sphinx.   A useful piece of work done by him was to
remove the sand which almost buried this mighty figure
and prevented people from fully appreciating its size.

Following Thothmes IV. comes Amenhotep III., in
whose reign architecture and sculpture arrived at a
high pitch of perfection.   He was a great warrior, and

[1] See 'Cleopatra's Needle,' By-paths of Bible Knowledge, No. 1.

the sculptures represent him receiving tribute of all
sorts from the people of Mesopotamia and Ethiopia.
In the former land he says that he killed two hundred
and ten lions with his own hand. He is renowned
also for the famous statues of Memnon, about 68 feet
high, which he erected before the palace of Luxor ;
one of these was broken by an earthquake a few years
before our era, and was afterwards repaired by the
Emperor Severus about 190 A.D. Before this accident
it was alleged that the figure sang when the rays of the
sun fell upon it at dawn.   Amenhotep III. was a devout
worshipper of the god Amen, and during his reign he
built a large number of temples to this god and to
others.   Amenhotep III. made his son, Amenhotep
IV., king during his own reign.   He is famous as
having been the introducer of the worship of the sun's
disk.   According to the Egyptian priests, he was an
unbeliever of the rankest type, for the most popular
worship at that time was that of the god Amen.   He
seemed to have taken such a dislike to this god, that he
changed his name from Amen-hotep to *Khu-en-aten*,
i.e., 'the glory of the disk ;' and not content with this, he
gave orders to have the name Amen erased from all the
sculptures, and he determined to remove from the
capital city and found a new one for himself, where he
could erect temples to his favourite deity.   In this place,
which is known to-day by the name of Tel-el-Amarna,
he built a magnificent temple in honour of the sun's
disk, not far from the Nile on the eastern side.   The

next important kings of this dynasty were called Ai and
Har-em-hebi : but we pass on at once to the important
nineteenth dynasty.

From the monuments we learn very little about
Rameses, the first of that name, and the founder of the
nineteenth dynasty (about 1400 B.C.). From later sources
he is known to have joined battle with Saprer the king
of the Khita or Hittites, but of this we shall speak
further on ; his battles with the Khita and other nations
were continued by his son Seti I. Seti took up arms
against the Asiatics, and made war with the Shasu or
Arabs, the Libyans and the Ethiopians : in the sculptures
we see him not only directing the battle, but at
times fighting hand to hand in mortal combat. The names
of the towns and fortresses were abolished by him, and
new Egyptian names given in their stead ; new fortresses
were built where necessary, and great pains were taken
to systematically reduce the countries around to the rule
of the king. Among the names of the places to which
he went are many which are met with in the Bible,
such as Canaan, Migdol, and Kadesh. He built the
Memnonium, a small temple to Sekhet at Beni-Hassan,
a well in the desert, and set up in Heliopolis an obelisk,
which is now in Rome, as well as many other great
works. He reigned fifty-one years, and the visitor to
Sir John Soane's Museum in Lincoln's Inn Fields may
there see his beautiful marble sarcophagus.

If Seti I. made Egypt great at home and abroad, it
was only a fitting preparation of the country for the long

and brilliant reign of his successor

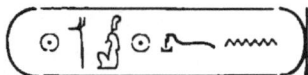

Rameses II. Under his rule the wars were carried out on
a larger scale than had ever before been contemplated ;
countries where the Egyptians had never been seen,
learned to know them by the soldiers of Rameses ; and
at home the arts and sciences advanced with such magnificent strides, that the civilised nations of to-day have
not yet ceased to wonder at the ingenuity and skill which
performed such wonderful deeds and works. Josiah
the king of Judah began to reign at the age of eight
years,[1] and it is probable that Rameses the Great was
at an equally early age associated with his father in the
rule of the kingdom : only four or five years after this
association he was already a man of war, having led an
expedition against the enemies of Egypt and beaten
them ; but, as we shall see soon, the youthful king had
the utmost need of all his power and bravery to keep
in check the immense number of nations which had
been rendered tributary to Egypt.

The first war in which the young prince took part
was that against the Ethiopians ; and in the fifth year
of his reign the brave rebellion of the Khita or Hittites
took place, which ended in the Khita being reckoned a
nation of almost equal importance with the Egyptians.
This war and its incidents have formed the subject of
the prize poem of a scribe called Pentaur, and although
Rameses II. did not come out of this fight with such

---

[1] 2 Kings xxii. I.

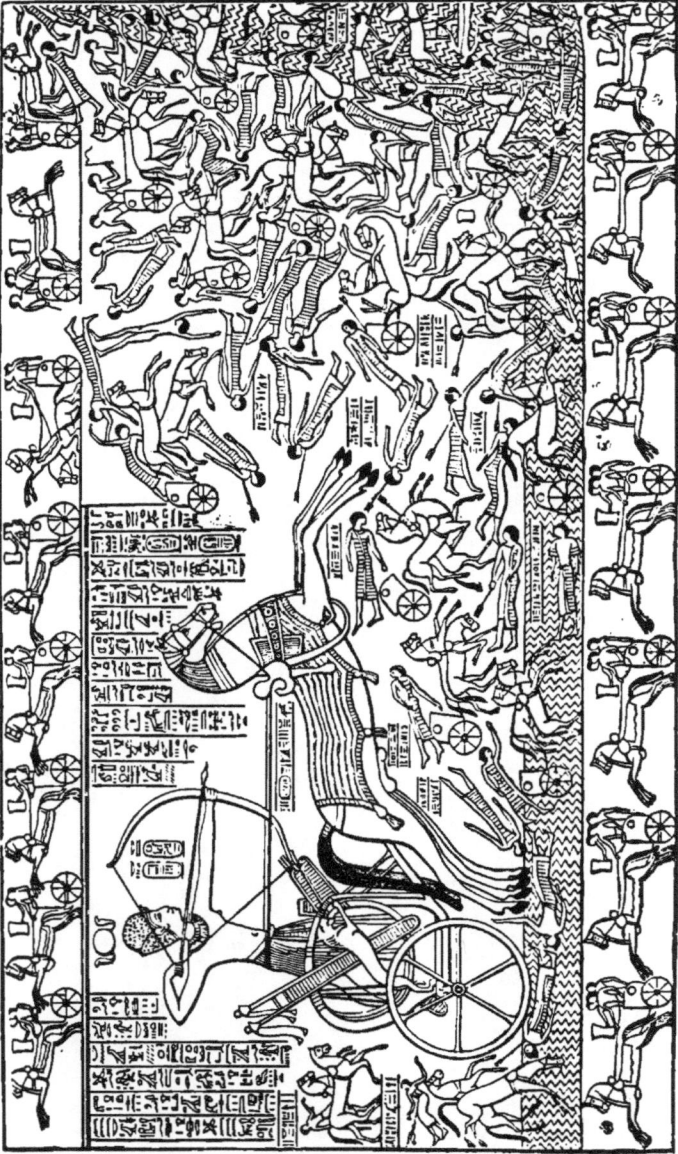

Rameses II. in Battle.

glory as he wished, yet the words of this song describing the bravery and deeds of the king in the highest terms of praise, were inscribed upon the walls of the temples at Abydos, and copies of it were made upon papyrus, to be handed down to future generations. Rameses II. was obliged to make a treaty with the Khita,[1] a copy of which, mutilated in some parts, is still extant.

Mr. Lushington's translation of the poems of Pentaur on the war will be found in the chapter on Egyptian literature, p. 100.

Not only in writing was this battle of Rameses II. celebrated, but the best artists of the day were employed to depict its various incidents at Abu-Simbel, Beit Oually, and elsewhere. At Kadesh on the Orontes a very fierce battle took place, and both sides fought with the greatest courage. The chariots of the Khita and their allies are depicted as having been overturned into the river. This battle cost them a number of very important lives : for the brother of the king of the Khita, the charioteer of the king, the chief general of the army, and the leader of the cavalry were all killed. One of the pictures shows the king of Khilibu or Khiribu, an ally of the Khita king, being rescued by his own men from drowning in the river. From the

---

[1] A translation of this document was first made by Rosellini in 1839 ; another by De Rougé in 1866 ; and a third by Goodwin in 1862. English versions are given in Brugsch's ' Egypt under the Pharaohs,' vol. ii., p. 68 ; and in Prof. Sayce's 'Fresh Light from the Ancient Monuments,' pp.191–197.

description of the battle we learn that Rameses advanced too far into the thick of the fight, and so found himself surrounded on all sides. In this difficulty and dire necessity the king prayed to Amen, who appearing to him, encouraged him with words, and taking him by the hand, led him to victory over the foe. So ended this great war; but whether Egypt gained much more than glory by it, is difficult to say. The treaty between Egypt and the Khita was, however, in later days firmly cemented by Rameses marrying, in his thirty-fourth year, the daughter of the king of the Khita, who took the Egyptian name of Ur-mā-neferu-Rā.

After the battle with the Khita Rameses in a series of wars reduced the Canaanites, the Amorites, the people of Syria, and others. He was a mighty builder, and erected temples to the principal gods of Egypt at Memphis, Thebes, and Abydos: he completed the great wall from Heliopolis to Pelusium, which his father Seti I. had begun to build, in order to keep out the never quiet Asiatics, who for ever desired to make inroads on the land of Egypt. It was on this wall that the 'treasure cities' of Pithom and Raamses,[1] which the children of Israel built, are supposed by some to have been placed; but other scholars have placed Pithom elsewhere, and identified the Hebrew Succoth with a district of Egypt called *Thuku*. In the latter part of his reign Rameses II. erased his father's name from the monuments, inserting his own in its place: the reader

[1] Ex. i. 11.

will remember that this king caused his name to be inscribed on two of the faces of 'Cleopatra's Needle,' while the other two bear the name of the king Thothmes III. who erected it. Rameses II. reigned sixty-seven years ; as co-regent with his father Seti I. for more than one-half of the time, and the remainder of the period as sole monarch. The monuments inform us that he had several wives, and one hundred and sixty-two children, of whom one hundred and eleven were sons. He was succeeded by his thirteenth son, called Mer-en-Ptaḥ, or Meneptah, who is remarkable for neither wars nor buildings, but who calls for our attention as being in all probability the 'Pharaoh' of the Exodus.

CHAPTER IV.

ILLUSTRATIONS OF THE PENTATEUCH AND BIBLE PASSAGES FROM THE EGYPTIAN MONUMENTS.

THE first of the Hebrew patriarchs who had intimate dealings with the Egyptians was the Chaldean Abraham. From his eastern home he wandered towards the West, and under the guidance of El-Shaddai the already aged man directed his journey to Canaan. During his journey through this land his God appeared to him,[1] and declared the promise that his seed should be its possessors. Now Abraham journeyed on towards the south.[2] Centuries must have elapsed since Egypt had become a settled monarchy with absolute monarchs, and a regular system of rule prevailed over the land. The care with which the Nile inundation was watched, how its waters were used for the irrigation of the country, the fertility of the land, its immense resources and its riches; the report of all these things would become the common property of the nations around, and hence the stranger Abraham journeying through Canaan would hear that even though there was a scarcity of food in Canaan, there was a certainty of food in Egypt. So towards Egypt he bent his steps,

[1] Gen. xii. 7.   [2] Gen. xii. 9.

meaning to remain there for a time.[1]   But the patriarch dreaded lest his wife should be taken from him, and lest himself should be slain.[2]   The possibility of such a thing being done has made some argue that the manners of the Egyptians must have been savage and barbaric. In the inscriptions, however, we meet two facts which bear upon this point; the first is recorded in the 'Tale of Two Brothers,' where we are told that a king of Egypt sent two armies to bring a beautiful woman to him, and to murder her husband; and the second is a statement in a papyrus pointed out by M. Chabas, which states that the wife and children of a foreigner are by right the lawful property of the king.   The kindness of the Pharaoh of Abraham is too well known to need any mention, and after receiving rich presents the patriarch went up out of Egypt.

It has been very generally supposed that Abraham's visit to Egypt took place under the reign of one of the kings of the twelfth dynasty, but *which* king has not yet been satisfactorily made out.   Egypt, like every country where the supply of water is irregular, was exceedingly liable to terrible famines, and history tells us that it was Amenemḥā III. who was the first king that appreciated the full danger of this calamity, for he gave all his attention to building the huge reservoir called Lake Moeris in the Fayoum.   Connected with this lake was a series of locks, dykes, and channels, by which the whole land might receive a regulated supply

---

[1] Gen. xii. 10.   [2] Gen. xii. 12.

F

of water. Even modern engineers have admired the
remains of this construction, and it has been said that
the Egypt of to-day would be a great gainer if the work
could be restored, and a new lake made.   Hence some
Biblical critics have considered that Amenemḥā III.
was king of Egypt when Abraham came there, and
others that Usertsen I. was king, and that Amenemḥā
was the Pharaoh of the time of Joseph ; but in any case
the fact that Abraham came there *about* that time is
generally accepted.

The next and most important of all the relations
which ever existed between the Jews and Egyptians,
was that begun by the arrival of Jacob's darling child
in Egypt.   Sold by his brethren to a company of Ish-
maelites for twenty pieces of silver,[1] he was in turn sold
by them in Egypt to Potiphar, an officer of Pharaoh's,
and the captain of the guard or executioners.   Here the
youthful and handsome Hebrew showed his devotion to
his master, and eventually became so trusted that he
was set over all his house.   The next part of his history
is illustrated by an extract from the D'Orbiney Papyrus
in the British Museum, containing the Story of the Two
Brothers.[2]   The papyrus was written by the scribe
Enna, and was originally in the possession of Seti II.,
a king of the nineteenth dynasty, so that it is as old as
the stay of the Jews in Egypt. A paraphrase of the
whole story is given in the chapter on Egyptian literature, p. 115.

[1] Gen. xxxvii. 28.   [2] See ' Records of the Past,' ii. p. 137.

When Potiphar had heard his wife's story, Joseph was cast into prison, where again he held a superior position, and where he interpreted the dreams of the butler and baker, the former of whom was pardoned on the king's birthday.   Later he is called upon to interpret the dreams of Pharaoh.   In all these narratives we find passages in which the testimony of the Bible and of the monuments go hand in hand.   Cups such as the king would have taken his wine from are portrayed ; baskets such as the baker would have carried his 'bakemeats' in are used even unto this day, and may be seen in the British Museum.   We know from the Rosetta Stone (line forty-six of the Greek text) that as late as that period (195 B.C.) it was customary to make great rejoicings on the king's birthday,[1] to consider it holy, and to do no work on it, and that the Pharaoh would pardon his butler as an act of grace is more than probable.

In the seven cows which Pharaoh saw feeding in the meadow, Dr. Birch has seen a reference to the seven cows of Athor, pictured in the vignette of the one hundred and forty-eighth chapter of the Book of the Dead ; and the Hebrew Bible has preserved the Egyptian word for 'reed grass' in the word which has been translated 'meadow.'

During the period of Pharaoh's anxiety to have his dreams interpreted, the butler remembered his former prison companion, Joseph, and made mention of him to

[1] Wilkinson, 'Ancient Egyptians,' iii. p. 330.

his lord. Before Joseph entered the presence he shaved,
and changed his raiment.[1]   Here again the monuments
and profane history offer us illustrations.   The Egyptians
only allowed their hair to grow during the times of
mourning, and to neglect the hair was considered very
slovenly and dirty; when a man of low station had
to be represented, the artist always drew him with a
beard. The artists carried this so far, that Rameses

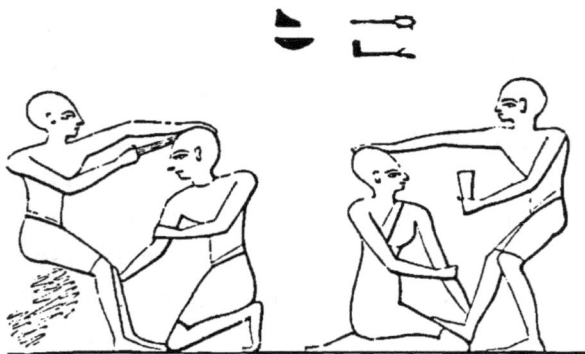

Egyptian Barbers at Work.

VII., who was negligent about his dress, is portrayed on
his tomb at Thebes with the addition of a stubbly
beard of some few days' growth. The heads of the
Egyptians were shaved, only locks being left here and
there, and the priests shaved the whole body every three
days, while the Jews and other foreign nations delighted
in long beards.   The British Museum possesses Egyptian
razors, and in a tomb at Beni-Hassan the act of shaving

[1] Gen. xli. 14.

is actually represented. The razors are of various shapes, and were carried about in a bag from place to place. The scribe who wrote the hymn in praise of learning has contrasted the hard work of the barber with that of the scribe. The scribe holds places of honour; from his youth he is a counsellor, and is sent on royal commissions; but

The barber is shaving till evening.
When he places himself to eat he places himself on his elbows.
He places himself at street after street
to seek after shaving.
He wearies his hands to fill his belly,
as bees feed by their labour.[1]

When Pharaoh had told his dream, and had heard its interpretation, he determined to accept the advice given by Joseph, and straightway appointed him lord over all Egypt, second only to the king, at the same time giving him rich and valuable presents. He first gave him a ring, the supreme emblem of the king's authority, which by that gift was transferred to Joseph; he next arrayed him in fine linen, for which Egypt was so celebrated, and which was the material of which the dress of the Egyptian priests was made; and putting a chain of gold about his neck, he made him ride through the land as ruler, while all the people shouted before him words of praise. The gift of a chain or collar of

[1] Dr. Birch, 'Records of the Past,' viii. p. 148.

gold to a high officer was apparently a custom with the
kings of Egypt.   When Ȧḥmes, the chief of the sailors,
and afterwards king of Egypt, cut off the head of a dead
enemy at Avaris and brought it to the king, a collar of
gold was given to him as a reward ; and after another
battle, in which he had shown the same prowess, he
received another chain or collar from the hands of the
grateful king.   The word or words which the Egyptians
cried out before Joseph offer much difficulty of
explanation ; some have said that they should be translated ' Bow the head,' and others think it means ' Rejoice ;'
but so far its real meaning is a mystery, though, should
the word be Hebrew, the rendering ' Bow the knee' is
probably good.   Besides all this, Pharaoh gave Joseph
an Egyptian name, and he married Asenath, the
daughter of a priest of On.   The name of his former
master, Potiphar, appears to be a perfectly good Egyptian
name, and Egyptologists have pointed out that its
probable equivalent in hieroglyphics is :—

i.e., ' devoted to the Sun-god.'

Pa-ṭa-pa-Rā

So likewise has Joseph's new name Zaphnath-paancah
been shown by Mr. Le Page Renouf and others to be

i.e., ' Storehouse of the house
of Life.'[1]

t'eft-ent-pa-ānχ

---

[1] Brugsch makes it, ' Governor of the district of the place of Life.'
—' Egypt under the Pharaohs,' ii. p. 265.

The name of his wife, Asenath, is said to mean 'devoted to Neit,' while the city On is the Annu, ⌂ or Heliopolis of the Egyptians. The gift of a new name to Joseph reminds us of Daniel being called Belteshazzar by Nebuchadnezzar, and the new names of Hananiah, Azariah, and Mishael ; while a parallel case of a foreigner being raised to so high a position in Egypt is given by the papyrus relating to the story of Saneha. The subsequent history of Joseph, his divining cup, his giving his brethren changes of garments, the land of Goshen being set apart for his father and brethren, because the shepherd was an abomination to the Egyptians, and the embalming of his father, exhibit in a striking manner the rigid accuracy of the Bible in its many references to Egyptian habits and customs.

Joseph would, of course, be held in the highest honour by the Pharaoh and his successors for the wonderful policy by which he 'bought all the land of Egypt for Pharaoh ;' and he proved beyond all doubt that it was possible for the crops of the years of plenty to be stored up, so that the inhabitants of the land should not perish in the years of drought or scarcity. So when we read that the people said to Joseph, 'Thou hast saved our lives,'[1] we must understand that it was not said with the lips only and without meaning ; but that it was the truth, and represented the heartfelt and grateful thanks

[1] Gen. xlvii. 25.

of a native to the man who was, as his Egyptian name
signified, ' the storehouse of the house of Life.'

After the days had multiplied, and the good and
great things which Joseph had done for Egypt had been
forgotten by the ruling dynasty, ' there arose up a new
king over Egypt, which knew not Joseph.'[1]   It is
generally accepted now that Joseph was sold into Egypt
at the time when the Hyksos were in power; and
it is also generally accepted that the Exodus took
place after the death of Rameses II., and under the
reign of Merenptah or Meneptah.   Now the children of
Israel were in captivity in Egypt for four hundred,[2] or
four hundred and thirty years;[3] and as they went out of
Egypt after the death of Rameses II., it was probably
some time about the year 1350 B.C.

There is little doubt that the Pharaoh who persecuted
the Israelites so shamefully was Rameses II.; though
there are some who say that it was Àḥmes or Amāsis I.
The Pharaoh first set the Israelites hard and difficult
burdens, and then appointed overseers to look after them
and see that they did their work.   Both tradition and the
monuments prove and supplement this statement; for
Diodorus[4] tells us that Rameses II. or Sesostris put up
an inscription in each of his buildings saying that it had
been erected by captives, and that not a single native
Egyptian was employed on the work.   Again, this king
set up a brick factory, or field as we should say, and by

[1] Ex i. 8.   [2] Gen. xv. 13.
[3] Ex. xii. 40.   [4] i. 56; Herod. ii. 108.

employing the labour of captives and others was enabled
to sell his bricks at a lower price than any other maker.[1]
Rameses II., like Nebuchadnezzar and the other kings of
Babylon, had a stamp made, and his
bricks were impressed with it.[2] They
were made with or without straw, and
it was a common custom not to burn
the bricks, but to dry them in the
sun ; for in that dry country, where
rain seldom comes, the sun-dried
brick was just as useful for the purpose of building as the baked. The
Jews appear to have lived upon their
own land, and some members of each
family no doubt tilled it, that the
others might have food. They were not the only nations
so employed, for the monuments show us people who
are certainly not Jews making bricks and performing
other servile work. They worked in detachments,
each superintended by a taskmaster, and they were
compelled to make so many bricks per day.[3] When
Pharaoh wished to increase their labour, he ordered
them to use stubble instead of straw, and so the already
overtasked labourers were obliged to go into the fields
where the reapers had been, and to cut off the stalks

BRICK STAMP OF
RAMESES II.

---

[1] Wilkinson, ' Ancient Egyptians,' i. p. 343.

[2] Sun-dried bricks of Rameses II., Thothmes III., &c., may be seen in
the British Museum (first Egyptian Room) ; as also a piece of burnt brick
of Thothmes III.

[3] Ex. v. 13.

that remained, to chop them small, and then to mix them with the mud. Whatever the Pharaoh ordered had to be done. Dr. Birch mentions the endorsement of a papyrus referring to twelve brick-makers employed to build a house, where it is said, ' Let there be no relaxation that they should make their number of bricks daily in the new house in the same manner, to obey the messages sent by my lord.' So then, together with slaves of other nations, the Jews were forced to build for their oppressor the treasure cities of Pithom and Raamses.[1] The town Raamses was called after the name of its builder Rameses II. ; and the remains of a town called Pithom—whose name means the 'Temple of Tmu '— have been found by M. Naville at a place which the monuments there call *Thuku* or *Thukut*, and which is said to be the Succoth of the Old Testament. There are difficulties in the way of accepting this theory, but their discussion here would be tedious to the non-expert, and quite out of place.

---

[1] We have in a papyrus a description of the happy town of Raamses contained in a poem, the concluding lines of which run :—

> There is a supply of provisions there daily.
> Gladness dwells within it.
> None speak scorn of it.
> There are sweet drinks in Aa-nechtu ;
> its liquors are like sugar,
> its syrups like the taste of
> caroobs surpassing honey.
>
> .   .   .   .   .
>
> Joy remains there prolonged, unceasing.
> Rameses, the war-god of the world, is its god

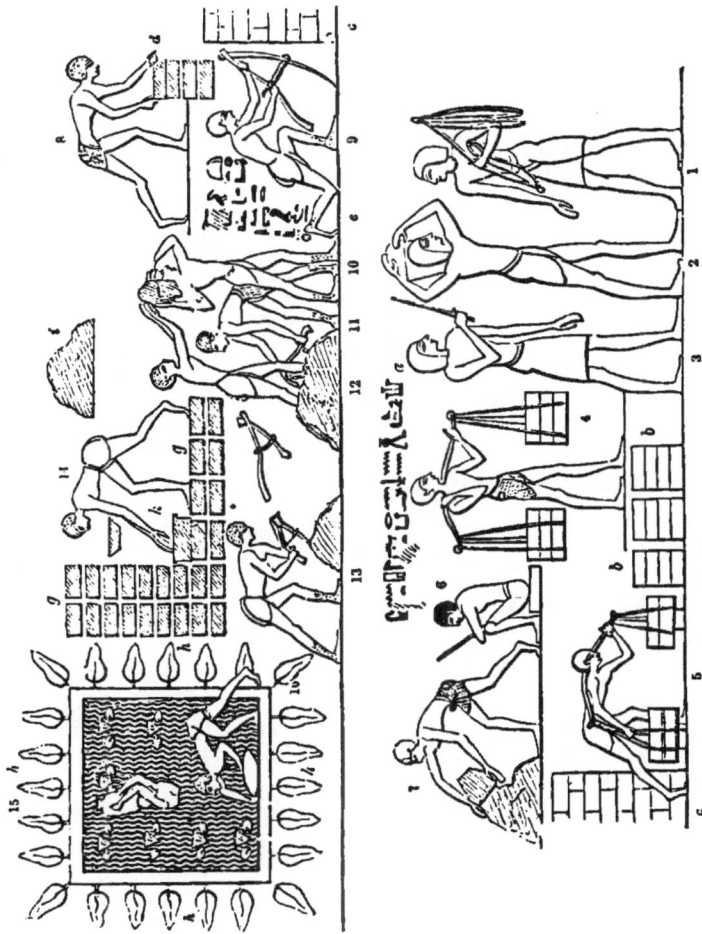

Egyptian Brickmakers and Brickmaking.

1. Man waiting to be laden. 3, 6. Taskmasters. 4, 5. Men carrying bricks. 8, 14. Stacking the moulded bricks. 9. Digging the clay
10. Man laden with prepared clay. 11. Mixing the clay. 15. Tank for water

In addition to the cruelty already exercised toward the children of Israel, the Pharaoh next gave orders to throw all the new-born male children into the river Nile : though, in spite of all the watchfulness employed in this matter, the child Moses was saved by being put in an ark of bulrushes, and laid among the reeds of the river.   This ark was made of the papyrus plant, and it has been pointed out that the mother made the ark of this substance because it was imagined by the Egyptians to be a preservative against the attacks of crocodiles and other noxious beasts.   When Pharaoh's daughter found the child, she decided to adopt it and bring it up ; and there can be little doubt that the future of the Jewish nation was much influenced by her act.   As soon as he was of a sufficient age he would be sent to the Egyptian schools ; there he would learn all that the most celebrated and profound masters of the day could teach : and after some years he would return, being skilled in writing and mathematics, and learned in all matters relating to the Egyptian religion, including its numerous branches of legend, myth, and history.   The manners and customs of the best of the Egyptians would be familiar to him, as well as the rules of government : and such learning was a fitting help for his divine mission, as it enabled him to fight Pharaoh with his own weapons, while it taught the great deliverer of his race how to rule, and judge, and to provide for the necessities of the people of Israel in future days.

There is no direct mention of the Israelites on the

monuments or in the papyri, it is true, neither is there
any representation of their servitude ; but it will be seen
from what has been said above that the references and
allusions in the Bible to Egypt and the Egyptians are
perfectly accurate. The Āmu, the representatives of the
Semitic race generally, are depicted as brick-makers,
and literally hewers of wood and drawers of water : hence
none need expect that every family or tribe of this
numerous and wide-spreading race would be portrayed
on the temples, or walls, or tombs. Also, there is no
mention of the plagues which came upon the oppressors ;
but the nations of antiquity were not given to chronicling
the misfortunes that overtook them. The persecution
which Rameses II. began was continued with vigour by

Meri-en-Ptah or Meneptah

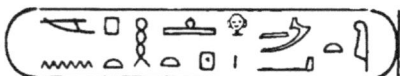

The bricks had to be made just the same, and the
appointed 'tale' brought at the end of the day. Relying
upon the long-sufferance and the captivity of the hosts
of Israel, he increased their burdens, and made their
lives so hard that their groans mounted up to the
throne of God. The edict of deliverance came, the
people went out in haste, but with riches, and the heart-
hardened Pharaoh and the chiefs of his host were
destroyed. The route of the Exodus has been a
subject of much discussion and much conjecture ; but it
will suffice to say that each of the theories hitherto laid
down offers many difficulties, and a mere enumeration

of them here would occupy much space, and give no
satisfactory result.

After Israel had gone forth out of Egypt, for some
two or three centuries there were no friendly relations
between the two nations until Solomon's time, when we
are told that 'Solomon made affinity with Pharaoh king
of Egypt, and took Pharaoh's daughter, and brought her
into the city of David ;'[1] but meanwhile the twentieth
dynasty had enjoyed its rule, and made way for the
twenty-first dynasty, whose first king was called
Harhor or Herher, and was a priest of the god Amen.
The Egyptians again come in contact with Israel under
the reign of Sheshank, or Shishak, the first king of the
twenty-second dynasty. 'In the fifth year of King
Rehoboam, Shishak king of Egypt came up against
Jerusalem, because they had transgressed against the
Lord, with twelve hundred chariots, and threescore
thousand horsemen : and the people were without
number that came with him out of Egypt ; the Lubims,
the Sukkiims and the Ethiopians. And he took the
fenced cities which pertained to Judah, and came to
Jerusalem.'[2] A list of the towns captured by Shishak
is given on a wall at Thebes ; and among them we find
Bethhoron, Ajalon, Megiddo, Edom, and 'Judah-melek,'
which Dr. Birch considers to be the royal city of Judah,
i.e., Jerusalem.[3]

By the time of the twenty-fifth dynasty Egypt had

[1] 1 Kings iii. 1.   [2] 2 Chron xii. 2-4.
[3] 'History of Egypt,' p. 157.

become divided into a number of small principalities,
which the Ethiopian prince Pi-ankhi ruled over at
Noph.[1] During the latter years of his reign, a rebellion
of the native princes, headed by Nimrod the prince of
Hermopolis, the chief of Menouthes, and others, broke
out; but the Ethiopian prince assembled his forces,
and having beaten the rebels in a series of successful
battles, he became lord of all Egypt. Concerning
Tirhakah,[2] a successor of Pi-ankhi, we derive very
important information from the Assyrian inscriptions.
Tirhakah had been defeated by Esarhaddon, who had
divided the country of Egypt into a number of districts,
generally under Egyptian governors ; some of the rulers
were, however, Assyrian, and a few of the Egyptian
towns were re-named with Assyrian names. Tirhakah
had incited the king of Tyre to rebel against the Assyrian
authority, and hence he brought down upon himself
Esarhaddon's attack, which resulted in his subjugation in
the twenty-third year of his reign. The Ethiopian
kings had offered help to the Jewish nation if they
would resist the Assyrians ; but Egypt's growing
weakness was well known, for Rab-shakeh, remembering
the successful attacks that Shalmaneser had made
against dependencies of Egypt, taunted Hezekiah with
the forlornness of any hope which was based upon

---

[1] Is. xix. 13 ; Jer. ii. 16 ; xlvi. 14, 19 ; Ezek. xxx. 13–16.
[2] The Tirhakah of 2 Kings xix. 9 ; Is. xxxvii. 9 ; and the
of the hieroglyphs.

Egyptian assistance, and compared Egypt's king to
'a bruised reed.'[1]   In the beginning of the reign of
Assurbanipal, Esarhaddon's son, Tirhakah made another
attempt to become sole king of Egypt; and having
collected a large army he entered Memphis and scattered
the Assyrian rulers.   Assurbanipal marched promptly
against the rebel, and defeated him with great slaughter.
Tirhakah then fled to Napata, where he with others
made arrangements for another rebellion; and he
succeeded so well that he conquered Upper Egypt, and
actually gained possession of Thebes.   Assurbanipal
sent an army against him, and Tirhakah was compelled
to retire to Napata, where he died, and so the twenty-
fifth dynasty came to an end.

Two of the kings of the next dynasty are mentioned in
the Bible, Pharaoh Necho and Pharaoh
Hophra.   The first met Josiah, king of Judah,
in battle at Megiddo, where Josiah was slain, and set
up Jehoiakim as king in the place of Josiah's eldest son
Jehoahaz, the lawful heir.   His power was, however,
broken by Nebuchadnezzar II., king of Babylon, and
we read that 'the king of Egypt came not again any
more out of his land.'[2]   The second, Pharaoh Hophra,
assisted Jehoiakim and Zedekiah, kings of Judah, to rebel
against their lord, Nebuchadnezzar; but this was merely
inviting the conquest of Egypt at the hands of the
Babylonian king, and a few years after the prophecies of

[1] 2 Kings xviii. 21.   [2] 2 Kings xxiv. 7.

G

Ezekiel and Jeremiah regarding its destruction were
fulfilled.   During the reign of Psammetichus I. the great
temples at Sais, Thebes, Memphis and elsewhere were
repaired.   This king made use of the Greeks in the
battle-field, and after the wars gave them a settlement
near Bubastis.

There was one among the last kings who caused
the fast-fading light of Egypt's glory to flicker brightly,
and this was Amāsis II.   After his death the country
was invaded by Cambyses the Persian, who became
king, and was the first of the Persian dynasty of
Egyptian kings.   Their rule lasted for about one hundred
years ; and following them came a few Egyptian kings of
little importance ; their reigns were very short, and they
in their turn were succeeded by another Persian dynasty.
For some time past Egypt had ceased to be Egyptian ;
the various conquerors of the country had caused new
customs to spring up; the use of the old system of
hieroglyphics had now practically died out ; the national
spirit was broken, and from this time forward Egypt
was a dependency and tributary to whatever king
arose and had power to seize it.   The nation with a
history that numbered thousands of years, and the
country that had shed the light of civilization abroad
when those round about were steeped in barbarism and
ignorance, now sank into a darkness which obscured
and eventually swallowed up the glory and majesty of
the Pharaohs and their land.

CHAPTER V.

EGYPTIAN LITERATURE.

A LARGE portion of the literature of Egypt comes down to us in the shape of historical inscriptions graven upon pyramids, obelisks, walls of temples, and stelæ. The sentences are sometimes short and abrupt ; but frequently they have a kind of rhythm which is exceedingly fine, and, owing to the parallelism of the members, reminds us of many of the Psalms. If, however, we were obliged to depend upon stone sculptures for our idea of the Egyptian literature, we should not have an adequate idea of it at all. Though the early 'pyramid texts,' with their rubrics, reveal to us the inscriptions which were fitting for funereal monuments, they give us no idea of the wonderful fairy stories which we obtain from the papyri. We have already stated that the *hieratic* writing was the writing of the priests, and as the learning of Egypt was locked up in the breasts of this caste, we must look to their works to understand what the literature of the Egyptians was. It must not be imagined that the hieratic is the only sort of writing found on papyrus ; on the contrary, we find many papyrus copies of the Book of the Dead in hieroglyphs,

G 2

and about 700 B.C. in demotic also. Still, a very large number of the most interesting compositions are found on papyrus in hieratic, and we give a few specimens from the best of them. The first is a translation of the very celebrated prize poem by the scribe Pentaur, giving a thrilling account of the battle of Rameses II. with the Khita or Hittites. This prize poem was considered so fine that it was inscribed upon the walls of temples, and a large number of copies must have been made. A papyrus which the British Museum possesses contains a very complete copy of it. Professor Lushington's translation is as follows :—

The Poem of Pentaur on the Conquest of the Khiti by Rameses II.[1]

Several days after that King Rameses was in the town Rameses Miamon. Moving northward he reached the border of Katesh ; then marched onward like his father (Mentu, towards) Hanruta. The first brigade of Ammon, 'that brings victory of King Rameses' (accompanied him). He was nearing the town ; then the vile chief of Cheta came ; he gathered (forces) from the margin of the sea to the land of Cheta ; came all the Naharina, the Airatu, the Masu, the Kashkash, the Kairakamasha, the Leka, Katuatana, Katesh, Akarita, Anaukasa, the whole Mashanata likewise, nor left he silver or gold in his land, he stripped it of all his treasures (which) he brought with him. The vile chief of Cheta, with many allies accompanying him, lay ambushed to north-west of (Katesh). Now King Rameses was all alone, no other with

---

[1] Prof. Lushington's translation, in the 'Records of the Past,' ii. p. 61.

him, the brigade of Ammon marching after him ; the brigade
(of Ra ?) at the dyke west of the town Shabutuna ; the brigade
of Ptah in the centre, the brigade of Set on the border of the
land of Amairo. Then the vile Cheta chief made an (advance)
with men and horses numerous as sand ; they were three men
on a car, they had joined with every champion of Chetaland,
equipped with all war gear, in (countless numbers); they lay
in ambush hidden to north-west of the town Katesh ; then they
charged the brigade of Ra Harmachis in the centre, as they
were marching on, and were not prepared to fight. Foot and
horse of King Rameses gave way before them ; they then took
Katesh on the western bank of Hanruta ; this news was told to
the King ; then he rose as Mentu, he seized his arms for battle ;
he clutched his corslet like Bar in his hour ; the great horse
that bore him, 'Victory in Thebes' his name, from the stable
of Rameses Miamon, within the van. The King drew himself
up, he pierced the line of the foe, the vile Cheta ; he was all
alone, no other with him. When he advanced to survey
behind him, he found there encircled him 2,500 chariots
stopping his way out. Every champion of the vile Cheta ard
abundant lands with him of Airatu, of Maasu, of Patasu, and
of Kashkash, of Iriuna, of Katuatana, of Chirabu, of Akarita,
Katesh, Leka, they were three men on a car; they made (a
charge), there was no chief with me, no marshal, no captain
of archers, no officers ; fled were my troops and horse. I was
left alone of them to fight the foe. Then said King Rameses,
'What art thou, my father Ammon? what father denies his
son ? For have I done aught without thee ? Have I not
stepped or stayed looking to thee, not transgressing the
decisions of thy mouth, nor passing far astray beyond thy
counsels ? Sovran Lord of Egypt, who makest to bow down

the peoples that withstand thee ; what are these Amu to thy
heart ?   Ammon brings them low who know not God.   Have
I not made thee monuments very many ?   filled thy temple
with my spoils ?   built thee a house for millions of years ? given
treasures to thy shrine ? dedicated to thee all lands, enriched
thy sacrifices ?   I have slain to thee 30,000 bulls, with all wood
of sweet scent, good incense coming from my hand.   The
making of thy court completed, I have built thee great towers
of stone above thy gate, groves everlasting.   I brought thee
obelisks from Elephantine ;   it is I who had eternal stones
carried, guiding for thee galleys on the sea, conveying to thee
the labours of all lands.   When was it said such happened in
other time ?   Shame on him who opposes thy counsels, well
be to him who approves thee, Ammon.   What thou hast done
is from a heart of love ;   I call on thee, my father Ammon.
I am amid multitudes unknown, nations gathered against me ;
I am alone, no other with me ; my foot and horse have left me.
I called aloud to them, none of them heard ;   I cried to them.
I find Ammon worth more than millions of soldiers, 100,000
cavalry, 10,000 brothers and sons, were they gathered all in one.
No works of many men avail, Ammon against them.   I attain
that by the counsels of thy mouth, O Ra, not overstepping thy
counsels.   Lo, have I not done homage to the farthest ends of
the land ?'   My cry rang unto Hermonthis ; Ra heard when I
called, he put his hand to me, I was glad ; he called to me
behind ; ' . . . . Rameses Miamon, I am with thee,
I thy father Ra, my hand is with thee.   I am worth to thee
100,000 joined in one ; I am Sovran Lord of Victory, loving
valour ; if I find courage, my heart overflows with joy ; all my
doing is fulfilled.'   I am as Mentu, I shoot to the right, I seize
on my left, like Bar in his fury against them ; I find 2,500

chariots, I am amidst them, then were they overthrown before
my steeds; not one of them found his hand to fight, their
hearts shrank within them ; their hands all dropped, they knew
not how to shoot, they found no heart to grasp the spear; I
made them fall into the water as fall crocodiles, they tumbled
headlong one over another ; I slew them ; my pleasure was
that none of them should look behind him, nor any return ;
whoever falls of them he must not raise himself up.   Then the
vile chief of Cheta stood amid his army to see the prowess of
King Rameses.   The King was all alone, no soldiers with him,
no horse; he turned in dread of the King.   Then he made
his mighty men go in numbers, each one of them with cars,
they brought all war harness, the chief of Airatu, the chief of
Masu, the chief of Iriuna, the Leka, the chief of Tantani, the
Kashkash, the chief of Kairkamash, the Chirabu, the allies of
Cheta, all banded in one, 2,500 chariots.   Charging the midst
of them fiercer than flame, I rushed upon them, I was as Mentu ;
I let my hand taste them in a moment's space, I hew at them
to slay them in their seats ; each one of them called to his
fellow, saying, 'No mortal born is he whoso is among us, Set
the mighty of strength ; Bar in bodily form, verily whoever
comes close to him, his hand droops through all his frame, they
know not how to grasp bow nor spear when they have seen him.'

Coming to the junction of roads, the King pursued them as
a griffin.   I was slaying them, none escaped me ; I gave a call
to my foot and horse, saying, 'Be firm, be firm in heart, my
foot and horse; behold my victory.   I was alone, Tum (Ammon)
my support, his hand with me.'   Now when Menna my
Squire saw me thus encircled by many chariots, he cowered,
his heart quailed, great terror entered his limbs, he said to the
King, 'My gracious Lord, Prince revered, valiant exceed-

ingly, protector of Egypt in day of battle, verily we stand
alone amid the foe, how make a stand to save breath to our
mouth? how rescue us, King Rameses, my gracious Lord?'
The King said to his Squire, 'Courage, courage, my Squire, I
will pierce them as a hawk; I will slay and hew them, cast
them to the dust. What forsooth to thy heart are these Amu?
Ammon brings very low them who know not God, who brightens
not his face on millions of them.' King Rameses dashed into
the van, then he pierced the foe, the caitiff Cheta, six times,
one and all, he pierced them. I was as Bar in his season, prevailing over them I slew them, none escaped. Then the King
called to his archers and cavalry, likewise to his chiefs who
failed to fight. 'Naught profits full heart in you. Is there one
of them who did his duty in my land? Had I not stood as
Royal Master, ye were downstricken. I make Princes of you
always. I set son in his father's estate: if any evil comes on
Egypt, ye quit your service . . . . Whoever comes to make
petitions I always pay regard to his claims. Never any Royal
Master did for his soldiers what King Rameses has done for
you, I let you sit in your houses and your towns; ye have not
performed my hests, my archers and cavalry. I have given
them a road to their cities, ... Lo, ye have played
cowards all together, not one of you stood to aid me while I had
to fight. Blessed be Ammon Tum, lo, I am over Egypt as my
father Ra; there was not one of them to observe my commands
in the land of Egypt. O noble feat! for consecrating images
in Thebes, Ammon's city: great shame on that act of my foot
and horse, greater than to tell, for lo, I achieve my victories;
there was no soldier with me, no horseman; every land beholds
the path of my victories and might. I was all alone, no other
with me, no chiefs behind, no marshals, no captains of the

army, no officers, all peoples saw and will tell my name to limits of lands unknown. If any warriors, relics of my hand, remain, they will turn at seeing me ; if 10,000 of them come upon me, their feet will not stand firm, they will fly ; whoever would shoot straight at me, down dropped their arrows, even as they approached me. Now when my foot and horse saw, I was addressed as Mentu, the strong sword of Ra, my father, who was with me in time of need, he made all peoples as straw before my horses. They were marching one after another to the camp at eventide ; they found all the tribes through whom I pierced strewn in carnage, whelmed amid their blood, with all brave fighters of Cheta-land, with children and brothers of their chief. Morning lighted the field of Katesh ; no space was found to tread on for their multitude. Then my soldiers came glorifying our names to see what was done, my cavalry likewise, extolling my prowess. 'What a goodly deed of valour ! firm in heart, thou hast saved thy army, thy cavalry, son of Tum, framed by his arms, spoiling Cheta-land by thy victorious sword, Royal Conqueror, none is like thee. King fighting for his host on day of battle, thou great of heart, first in the fray, thou reckest not for all peoples banded together, thou great conqueror before thy army, in the face of the whole land. No gainsaying. Thou guardest Egypt, chastisest lands of thy foes, thou bruisest back of Cheta for ever.' Then the King addressed his foot and horse, likewise his chiefs who failed to fight : 'Not well done of one of you, your leaving me alone amid the foe ; there came no chiefs, officer or captain of host to aid me. I fought repelling millions of tribes all alone. "Victory in Thebes" and " Nehrahruta" (my horses) they are all I found to succour me. I was all alone in the midst of foes. I will let them eat corn before Ra daily, when I am in my royal palace : these are they found in the midst of the foe, and my Marshal Menna my Squire, with the officers of my household who were near me, the witnesses of conflict who saw them fall before the King; with victorious strength he felled 100,000 all at once, by his sword of might.' At dawn he joined in fray of battle ; he went terrible to fight, as a bull terrible with pointed horns he rose against them as Mentu ordering the fray, alike valiant in entering battle, fighting fierce as a hawk, overthrowing them as Sechet who sends flames of fire in the face of thy foes ; as Ra in his rising at the front of dawn, shooting flames upon the wicked ; one man amongst them calls to his fellow, ' Mark, take heed, verily Sechet the mighty is with him ; she guides his horses : her hand is with him.' Whoever approaches sinks to ruin ; she sends fire to burn their limbs, they were brought to kiss the dust. King Rameses prevailed over them, he slew them, they escaped not, they were overthrown under his steeds, they were strewn huddled in their gore. Then the vile Cheta Prince sent to do homage to the great name of King Rameses. ' Thou art Ra Harmachis, thou art Set mighty of strength, son of Nut, Bar himself; thy terror is over Cheta-land brought low : thou hast broken back of Cheta for ever and ever.' Then came a herald bearing a scroll in his hand to the great name of Rameses, ' To soothe the heart of the King, Horus, conquering Bull, dear to Ma, Prince guarding thy army, valiant with the sword, bulwark of his troops in day of battle, King mighty of strength, great Sovran, Sun powerful in truth, approved of Ra, mighty in victories, Rameses Miamon. The servant speaks to tell the King, My gracious Lord, fair son of Ra Harmachis, truly thou art born of Ammon, issue of his body, he gives thee all lands together, land of Egypt and land of Cheta, they offer their service beneath thy feet to thee, Ra, prevailing over them. Yea, thy spirit is mighty, thy strength weighs heavy on Cheta-land ; is it good to kill thy servants ? thou exercisest thy might upon them ; art thou not softened ? thou camest yesterday and slewest 100,000 of them ; thou art come to-day . . . . . victorious King, Spirit glad in battle, grant us breath of life.' Then the King rose in life and strength, as Mentu in his season. Then he bade summon all the leaders of foot and horse, his army all assembled in one place to let them hear the message sent by the great chief of Cheta to King Rameses. They answered, saying to the King, ''Tis very good to let fall thy wrath, Prince, Sovran Lord, ... who can soothe thee in thy day of anger ? ' Then King Rameses gave assent to their words ; he gave his hand in peace, returning to the South, passing in peace to Egypt with his chiefs, his foot and horse, in life and strength, in sight of all lands. Dread of his might is in every heart, he protects his army, all nations come to the great name, falling down and adoring his noble countenance. King Rameses reached fort Rameses Miamon great image of Ra Harmachis reposing in the royal palace in Thebes, as the sun's orbs, on his two-fold throne ; Ammon hailed his form, saying, ' Glory to thee, son loved of us, Rameses Miamon (to whom we grant) festivities for ever on the throne of thy father Tum. All lands are overthrown under his feet : he has quelled (all enemies).' Written in the year 7, month Payni, in the reign of King Rameses Miamon, giver of life for ever and ever like his father Ra . . . . To the Head Guardian of the royal writings . . . . . by the Royal Scribe Pentaur.

When the Egyptian wrote history, he related the facts clearly and concisely, and with but few unnecessary additions; these consist principally of the incessant repetition of the names and titles of honour of the Pharaohs.[1] It seems probable that the Egyptians did not write a compendium of the history of their nation, for as each king proclaimed his own works and glories upon his edifices and buildings, succeeding generations could read the history of the times before upon them : yet they forgot that dynasties are overthrown and monuments destroyed. If we had a *complete* native history of Egypt, however brief, what a number of unproven facts it would make certain !

It is evident that with a nation like the Egyptians, possessing such a number of gods, a very large portion of their works would turn upon religion and myths about the gods, hymns to them, and the like. To the Nile, as a god whose practical gifts would be apparent to all, would the pious Egyptian poet address his devotions. The two following extracts will show the reverence in which it was held. The hieroglyphs surrounding the pages are not part of the text of which the hymns are translations, but are given simply as an illustration of hieroglyphic text. They are taken from Maspero's ' La Pyramide du Roi Pepi Ier,' lines 163 and 164.

---

[1] As a specimen of this, see the first few lines of the translation of the Rosetta Stone on p. 22.

I.

Blessed be the good god,[1]
the Nun[2]-loving Nile,
the father of the gods of the holy Nine[3]
dwelling on the waters,
the plenty, wealth, and food of Egypt.
He maketh everybody live by himself,
riches are on his path,
and plenteousness is in his fingers ;
the pious are rejoiced at his coming.
Thou art alone and self-created,
one knoweth not whence thou art.
But on the day thou comest forth and
openest thyself,
everybody is rejoicing.
Thou art a lord of many fish and gifts,
and thou bestowest plenteousness on Egypt.
The cycle of the holy Nine knoweth not
whence thou art,
thou art their life.
For when thou comest their offerings are
redoubled,
and their altars filled,
and they are shouting when thou appearest.

---

[1] 'Records of the Past,' x. p. 37.
[2] *i.e.*, Heaven-loving.
[3] Shu, Tefnut, Seb, Nut, Osiris, Horus, Isis, Nephthys, and Set.

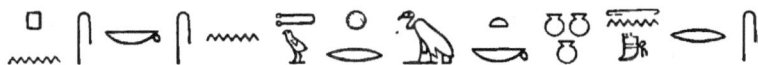

II.

He giveth light on his coming from dark-
ness ;[1]
in the pastures of his cattle
his might produceth all :
what was not, his moisture bringeth to life.
Men are clothed to fill his gardens :
he careth for his labourers.
He maketh even and noontide,
he is the infinite Ptah and Kabes.
He createth all works therein,
All writing, all sacred words,
All his implements in the North.
The hymn is addressed to thee with the
harp ;
It is played with a (skilful) hand to thee !
The youths rejoice at thee !
Thy own children.
Thou hast rewarded their labour.
There is a great one adorning the land ;
An enlightener, a buckler in front of men,
Quickening the heart in depression,
Loving the increase of all his cattle.
Mortals extol (him), and the cycle of gods !
Awe is felt by the terrible ones ;

---

[1] 'Records of the Past,' iv. p. 111.

his son (*i.e.* Pharaoh) is made Lord of all, to enlighten all
    Egypt.
Shine forth, shine forth, O Nile ! shine forth!
Giving life to his oxen by the pastures !
Shine forth in glory, O Nile.

But though the Nile was thus hymned and praised as
the giver of all good gifts and life to the Egyptians, the
highest and best praises were reserved for the great gods
of the Egyptian Pantheon.   The sun-god Rā, as the
giver of light and warmth to the world, the nourisher of
crops and the dispeller of darkness, was a favourite
theme for the Egyptian poet, and in combination with
other gods the most beautiful hymns, full of noble
epithets, were written in his honour ; as for example :—

Hail to thee Ra, Lord of truth :
whose shrine is hidden, Lord of the gods :
Chepera (*i.e.*, the Creator) in his boat :
at whose command the gods were made :
Atum, maker of men :
supporting their works, giving them life :
distinguishing the colour of one from another :
listening to the poor who is in distress :
gentle of heart when one cries unto him.
Deliverer of the timid man from the violent :
judging the poor, the poor and the oppressed :
Lord of wisdom whose precepts are wise :
at whose pleasure the Nile overflows :
Lord of mercy most loving :

    [1] See ' Transactions Soc. Bib. Arch.,' ii. p. 250.

at whose coming men live :
opener of every eye :
proceeding from the firmament :
causer of pleasure and light :
at whose goodness the gods rejoice
their hearts revive when they see him.

    *   *   *   *   *   *

Hail to thee for all these things :
the ONE alone with many hands !
lying awake while all men lie (asleep) :[1]
Amen, sustainer of all things :
Atum, Horus of the horizon :
homage to thee in all their voices ;
salutation to thee for thy mercy unto us ;
protestations to thee who hast created us.

III.

Thou wakest beauteous Amen-Rā-Harmachis, thou watchest in triumph, Amen-Rā, Lord of the horizon. O blessed one beaming in splendour, towed by thy mariners who are of the unresting gods, sped by thy mariners of the unmoving gods. Thou comest forth, thou ascendest, thou towerest in beauty, thy barge divine careers wherein thou speedest, blest by thy mother Nut each day, heaven embraces thee, thy foes fall as thou turnest thy face to the West of heaven. Counted are thy bones, collected thy limbs, living thy flesh, thy members blossom, thy soul blossoms, glorified is thy august form, advanced thy state on the road of darkness. Rā hath quelled his impious foes, heaven rejoices, earth is in delight, gods and goddesses are in festival to make adoration to Rā-Hor, as they

---

[1] Compare Psalm cxxi. 4.

H

see him rise in his bark. He fells the wicked in his season, the abode is inviolate, the diadem in its place, the uræus has smitten the wicked."[1]

Following close upon these religious hymns come the magical texts, the knowledge of which enabled its possessor to drive away a disease or devil. If medicine was taken to cure the disease, then an incantation or formula was said at the time of taking it, that the drug might do its work swiftly and well ; and if a man was under the power of one devil, the unfortunate prayed to another and mightier devil, or a god, to protect him from his power of injury. An extract from the translation of a magical text by Dr. Birch will give an idea of this class of work :—[2]

There are four mansions of life, Osiris is master thereof. The four houses are Isis, Nephthys, Seb, and Nu. Isis is placed in one, Nephthys in another, Horus in one, Tahuti in another, at the four angles ; Seb is above, Nu is below. The four outer walls are of stone. It has two stories, its foundation is sand, its exterior is jasper, one is placed to the south, another to the north, another to the west, another to the east. . . . . . Shu takes the shape of an eagle's wing ; he makes a lock or tress of sheep's wool to go round this god's neck ; it is placed on the throat of Osiris. Shu says : 'O thou shut in the solar disk, hidden in thy house ! O you enemies who retain the breath far from him turn your faces. A lock of hair has been made to suffocate your souls. I am Shu who destroys your bodies.'

[1] See full translation by Prof. Lushington, 'Records of the Past,' viii. p. 129.
[2] 'Records f the Past,' vi. p. 113

The Egyptian appears to have been very devoted to tales of the imagination ; for an instance we cannot do better than paraphrase the Tale of the Two Brothers.[1]

There were two brothers, children of one mother and of one father. Anpu was the name of the elder, Bata that of the younger. Anpu had a house and a wife, and his younger brother was like a son to him. He followed after the cattle, he did the ploughing and all the labours of the fields. Behold his younger brother was so good a labourer that there was not his equal in the whole land. Now while the younger brother was with the cattle every day in the fields, taking them home each evening, and while he was in the stables, the elder brother sat with his wife and ate and drank. And when the day dawned, and before his brother rose from his bed, he took bread to the fields and called the labourers to eat in the field. The cattle told him where the best grasses were, and he understood their language. And when it was the season for ploughing, the elder brother said, ' Come, let us take our teams for ploughing, for the land has made its appearance ; go and fetch seed for us from the village.' And the younger brother found the elder brother's wife sitting at her toilet. And he said, ' Arise and give me seed that I may go back to the field, because my elder brother wishes me to return without delay.' Then she said, ' Go open the bin, and take thyself whatever thou wilt, my hair would fall by the way.' So the youth entered his stable ; he took a large vessel, for he wished to take a great deal of seed, and he loaded himself with grain and went out with it. And she spoke to him saying, ' What strength is there in thee, indeed. I observe thy vigour every day.' She seized upon him and said,

---

[1] Renouf, ' Records of the Past,' ii. p. 136.

to him, 'Come let us lie down for an instant.' The youth
became like a panther with fury on account of the shameful
discourse which she had addressed to him.   He spoke to her,
saying, 'Verily I have looked upon thee in the light of a
mother, and thy husband in the light of a father to me.   What
a great abomination is this which thou hast mentioned to me.
Do not repeat it again to me, and I will not speak of it to any
one ; verily I will not let any thing of it come forth from my
mouth to any man.'

Behold, the wife of his elder brother was alarmed at the
discourse which she had held.   She made herself like one who
had suffered violence, for she wished to say to her husband,
'It is thy younger brother who has done me violence.'   Her
husband returned at evening and found his wife lying as if
murdered by a ruffian.   And she said, 'No one has conversed
with me except thy younger brother ; when he came to fetch
seed for thee, he found me sitting alone, and said insulting
words to me.   But I did not listen to him.   Behold am I not
thy mother, and thy elder brother is he not like a father to thee ?
This is what I said to him, and he got alarmed, and did me
violence that I might not make a report to thee ; but if thou
lettest him live I shall kill myself.'   And the elder brother
became like a panther ; he made his dagger sharp, and took it
in his hand, and placed himself behind the door of the stable
to kill his younger brother on his return at evening to bring his
cattle to the stable.

When the sun was set, the younger brother loaded himself
with the herbs of the field and came home.   And when the
first cow entered the stable she said to him, 'Verily thy elder
brother is standing before thee with his dagger to slay thee.
Betake thyself from before him.'   The second beast spake

after the same manner, and when he looked he saw the two feet of his elder brother who was standing behind the door ; and placing his burden upon the ground he fled. In his flight the young man prayed to the Sun-god, who straightway caused the two brothers to be divided by a river full of crocodiles, and each brother stood upon an opposite bank. At daybreak the younger brother declared his innocence, and told his brother the true story ; he then mutilated himself, and declared his intention of going to the Cedar mountains. But before going the younger tells the elder brother what will happen in the following words : ' I shall take my heart, and place it in the top of the flower of the Cedar, and when the Cedar is cut down it will fall to the ground. Thou shalt come to seek it. If thou art seven years in the search of it, let not thy heart be depressed, and when thou hast found it thou shalt place it in a cup of cold water. Oh ! then I shall live (once more), and fling back a reply to an attack. And this thou shalt learn, namely, that the things have happened to me. When thou shalt take a jug of beer into thy hand and it turns to froth, then delay not ; for to thee of a certainty is the issue coming to pass.' So the young man went to the Cedar mountain, and the elder brother went home. Arrived there, he strews dust upon his head, kills his wife and throws her to the dogs, and then mourns for his brother. Meanwhile the younger brother spent his time in hunting, and in building for himself a most beautiful house. And it fell out one day that the company of the gods met him, and one of them asked him why he stayed there alone, seeing that his brother's wife had been slain. Then they pitied him, and the god Chnum made him a wife, a most beautiful woman, in whom was the whole godhead ; but the seven Hathors when they saw her declared with one voice that

she would die a violent death. Then the days multiplied,
and they lived very happily together, and the young man said
to her before he went out hunting, 'Do not go out, lest the Sea
carry thee off, for my heart is on the top of the flower of the
Cedar, and if any one finds it I shall be overcome by him.' So
the young man hunted as usual, and one day while he was
away the Sea saw her and chased her; but she fled and
reached her house. And the Sea said to the Cedar, 'O that
I could seize upon her!' And the Cedar carried off one of
her fragrant locks and carried it to Egypt, and deposited it
where the washers of the king were. Then the odour of this
lock diffused itself among the king's clothes, and one day
when the chief of the washers was walking by the sea, he saw
the lock of hair, picked it up, and finding the odour exceedingly
delicious, he took it to the king. When the doctors and
magicians saw it they said, 'This lock belongs to a daughter of
the Sun-god; the essence of the whole godhead is in her. Send
envoys to every place to seek her, but send a number of troops
with the envoy who is to go to the Cedar mountain.' This was
done, and after a time all the envoys returned; but those who
had gone to the Cedar mountain returned not; for the young
man Bata had slain them. Then the king sent more troops to
the Cedar mountain, who brought back Bata's wife with them,
and she advised the king to cut down the Cedar, for then Bata
would be destroyed. So the Cedar was cut down, and Bata
fell dead.

The following day the elder brother Anpu went into his
house, and sat down to drink beer, but the beer in the jug
became froth; and when he saw the fulfilment of his younger
brother's prophecy he set out on a journey to the Cedar
mountain. When he came there he found his brother dead

upon the floor, and went out forthwith to look for his brother's heart under the Cedar where he used to lie in the evening. For three years he searched for the heart, and, quite disheartened, he determined to go back to Egypt; but going to take a final look at the place, he found a pod, and under the pod his brother's heart. He took the heart and dropped it into water, and the heart absorbed the water. When all the water had been drunk up, Bata, the younger brother, became alive, and the two brothers embraced each other. Bata said to his brother, Anpu, 'I am going to become a great bull with all the sacred marks; do thou sit upon my back, and when the Sun rises we shall be in the place where my wife is.' On the following day Bata became a bull, and he and his brother arrived at the place where his wife was. Then the king made a great festival and honoured the elder brother greatly. After a while the bull entered the sanctuary and stood near the princess, and said, 'Look upon me, I am alive indeed.' The Princess asked, 'Who art thou then?' He answered, 'I am Bata, I am a Bull.' Then she was horribly afraid, and one day when the king sat at meat with her she said, 'Come swear to me by God that you will grant whatever I ask.' The king promised, and she asked to eat the liver of the Bull. Then the king was sad, but all the same he gave orders to slay the bull. As they were killing him, two drops of blood fell upon the two door-posts; and they grew up into two mighty Persea trees, each of which stood alone. After some time the King and the Princess went out to see the Persea trees, and as the latter was sitting under one of them, it said, 'Ho! thou false one! I am Bata, I am living still, I have transformed myself.' At this the Princess asked to have the Persea trees cut down; and the King gave orders to have this done, while she looked on; but a splinter flew into her mouth. And after a time it was told the King, 'There is born to thee a male child.' When the child grew up he was made Prince of Ethiopia, and afterwards hereditary prince; and when the King died he summoned all the princes and nobles of his majesty and narrated all that had happened to him. His wife also was brought to him, and he had a reckoning with her in presence of them, and they spoke their speech. Then he appointed his elder brother Anpu to be hereditary prince, and he himself became king. And when he had completed thirty years of life, his elder brother arose in his place, on the day of his death.

Such is the brief account of the Tale of the Two Brothers. Another curious story is that of the Possessed Princess of Bakhten.[1] It appears that when Rameses XII. was in Mesopotamia registering the annual tributes of vassal princes, the chief of the land of Bakhten, in laying his gifts at the feet of the monarch, placed his eldest daughter first. This lady was very beautiful, and as she delighted the heart of his Majesty beyond all things, she was made chief royal wife, and called Rā-neferu, or 'the glories of the Sun-god.' One day after the king had returned, and was in Thebes, there came ambassadors from the country of Bakhten, who, together with the chief of that land, brought presents for the king's wife, their former princess. When the chief obtained an audience of his Majesty Rameses, he said, ' Glory, to thee, sun of the Nine bow barbarians, let us live

---

[1] For full translation by Dr. Birch, see ' Records of the Past,' iv. p. 53.

before thee.' He then went on to tell the king that he
had come on account of Bent-Rash, the little sister of Rā-
neferu, the king's wife, their former princess, for she had
become stricken with some evil movement in her limbs,
therefore would his Majesty send someone to heal her.
Rameses ordered all those learned in mysteries to
appear before him, and when they had come his choice
fell upon the royal scribe Tahuti-em-heb, who was
intelligent in heart and skilled with his fingers. This
learned man went to Bakhten, and when he had
examined the girl he found that she was under the
influence of evil spirits. He found the devils difficult to
contend with, and making a report to this effect he
wound up by asking that a god might be sent to
exorcise the demons. When the king received the
report he prostrated himself before the god Chonsu of
the double name in Thebes, and entreating his help,
prayed that the good god would consent to go to
Bakhten, to save the daughter of the prince of that land.
The god was gracious and expressed his readiness to go ;
then the king forthwith placed him in an ark, and the
god departed from the land. When he arrived in
Bakhten, the whole army, headed by the chief of the
land, made obeisance before him. The god then went
to the place where the child possessed of devils was, and
cured her immediately ; and the spirit which came out
from her spake to Chonsu, 'Thou, O great god, and
driver away of possessors, hast come in peace ; the land
of Bakhten is thy city; its men are thy slaves; I am thy

slave; I will go to the place whence I came, to give peace to thy heart on account of thy journey here.' After this speech the god requested that the Prince of Bakhten would offer sacrifice to the spirit that had come forth from his daughter. When this was done the spirit departed, as he had said. At this the Prince of Bakhten was so pleased with the god Chonsu that he determined to keep him there. The god stayed in Bakhten three years and a few months; but one night when the Prince was lying on his couch he saw the god in the form of a golden hawk come out of his shrine and fly away to the land of Egypt. After this the Prince sent the ark of the god away to Egypt with great and rich presents, troops and many horsemen.

The literature of Egypt embraced all subjects, if we may judge by what has come down to us: mathematics, police reports—like that which relates the criminal proceedings against some people who broke open and robbed some of the tombs of the kings—moral sayings, and many other subjects for which we have no room to give specimens here. We reserve a notice of the Book of the Dead for the ninth chapter, and will conclude our series of extracts from Egyptian literature by two most interesting poetical specimens. The first is from a very old work on the praise of learning,[1] and the second is the ' Song of the Harper.'[2] This latter work is inscribed upon a tomb at Abd-el-Gurnah, and the reader will see

[1] ' Records of the Past,' viii. p. 147.
[2] *Ibid.*, vi. p. 127.

that many of the passages in it are somewhat similar in meaning to verses in Ecclesiastes and other parts of the Bible :—

I.

I have seen violence, I have seen violence, give thy heart after letters.

I have seen one free from labours, consider there is not anything beyond letters.

Love letters as thy mother, I make its beauty go in thy face, it is a greater possession than all honours.

He who has commenced to avail himself is from his infancy a counsellor.

He is sent to perform commissions.

He who does not go, is in sackcloth.

I have not seen a blacksmith on a commission, a founder who goes on an embassy.

I have seen the blacksmith at his work at the mouth of the furnace.

His fingers like things of crocodiles, he stinks worse than the eggs of fishes.[1]

Every carpenter carrying tools, is he more at rest than the labourers ?

His fields are of wood, his tools of metal ; at night when he is free he does in addition work with his hands for the lighting of his house.[2]

---

[1] Compare, 'The smith also sitting by the anvil, and considering the ironwork, the vapour of the fire wasteth his flesh, and he fighteth with the heat of the furnace : the noise of the hammer and anvil is ever in his ears, and his eyes look still upon the pattern of the thing that he maketh ; he setteth his mind to finish his work, and watcheth to polish it perfectly' (Ecclesiasticus xxxviii. 28).

[2] Compare Ecclesiasticus xxxviii. 27.

The poet then proceeds to describe the difficulties of each trade, and finishes with :—

I tell you the fisherman suffers more than any employment.
Consider, is he not toiling on the river? he is mixed up with the crocodiles.
Should the clumps of papyrus diminish, then he is crying out for help.
If he has not been told that a crocodile is (not) there,
Terrors blind him.
Consider, there is not an employment destitute of superior ones.
Except the scribe, who is the first.   For he who knows letters, he then is better than thee.
Should'st thou walk after great men, thou art to proceed with good knowledge.
Do not say proud words.   Be sealed in thyself alone.

II.

The Song of the Harper.

[Chanted by the singer to the harp who is in the Chapel of the Osirian, the Patriarch of Amen, the blessed Neferhotep.]
   He says :
The great one is truly at rest,[1]
the good charge is fulfilled.[2]
Men pass away since the time of Rā,
and the youths come in their stead.[3]
Like as Rā reappears every morning,
and Tum sets in the horizon,

---

[1] Job iii. 17.   [2] 2 Tim. iv. 7.   [3] Eccles. i. 4.

men are begetting,
and women are conceiving.
Every nostril inhaleth once the breezes of dawn,
but all born of women go down to their places.

Make a good day, O holy father !
Let odours and oils stand before thy nostril.
Wreaths of lotus are on the arms and the bosom of thy sister, .
dwelling in thy heart, sitting beside thee.
Let song and music be before thy face,
and leave behind thee all evil cares !
Mind thee of joy, till cometh the day of pilgrimage,
when we draw near the land which loveth silence.[1]

Make a good day, O blessed Neferhotep,
thou Patriarch perfect and pure of hands !
He finished his existence .   .   .   .
Their abodes pass away,
and their place is not ;
they are as they had never been born
since the time of Rā.
(They in the shades) are sitting on the bank of the river,
thy soul is among them, drinking its sacred water,
following thy heart, at peace .   .   .   .
Give bread to him whose field is barren,
thy name will be glorious in posterity for evermore ;
they will look upon thee   .   .   .
(The priest clad in the skin) of a panther will pour to the
     ground
and bread will be given as offerings ;

[1] Eccles. iii. 13 ; v. 18 ; viii. 15 ; Is. xxii. 13 ; Wisdom of Solomon,
chap. ii.

the singing women . . . .
Their forms are standing before Rā,
their persons are protected . . .
Rannu will come at her hour,
and Shu will calculate his day,
thou shalt awake . . . . (woe to the bad one !)
He shall sit miserable in the heat of infernal fires.[1]

Make a good day, O holy father,
Neferhotep, pure of hands !
No works of buildings in Egypt could avail,
his resting-place is all his wealth . . . .
Let me return to know what remaineth of him !
Not the least moment could be added to his life,
(when he went to) the realm of eternity,
Those who have magazines full of bread to spend,
even they shall encounter the hour of a last end.[2]
The moment of that day will diminish the valour of the rich.
Mind thee of the day when thou too shalt start for the land,
to which one goeth to return not thence.[3]
Good for thee then will have been (an honest life),[4]
therefore be just, and hate transgressions,[5]
for he who loveth justice (will be blessed).
The coward and the bold, neither can fly (the grave),
the friendless and proud are alike . . .[6]
Then let thy bounty give abundantly as is fit,
(love) truth, and Isis shall bless the good,
(and thou shalt attain a happy) old age.

[1] Mark ix. 44.   [2] Luke xii. 18–21.
[3] The Assyrians also called Hades ' the land of no return ;' and it was there that Ishtar went to seek Tammuz.
[4] Ps. xxxvii. 37.   [5] Amos v. 15.   [6] Job iii. 14–19.

Isis and Horus.

Mut.

Basht.

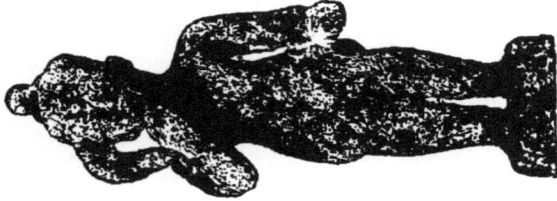

Harpocrates.

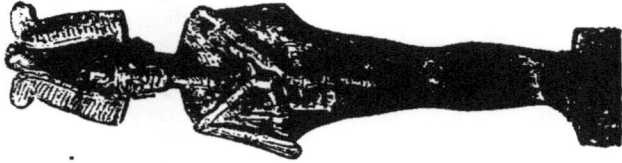

Osiris.

Pnebta.

GROUP OF EGYPTIAN GODS. *From Originals in the British Museum.*

CHAPTER VI.

The Egyptian Religion.[1]

THE number of gods which went to form the Egyptian Pantheon is at once surprising and confusing. Every nome possessed its god, and of course supported a number of priests to carry on its worship. In some places triads of gods existed; for example, at Thebes the triad was composed of Amen, Mut, and Chonsu; and at Abydos, of Osiris, Isis, and Horus. Often too we meet with groups of nine gods, and some texts in speaking of the gods repeat the sign for 'god' eighteen times, to indicate a double group of nine, or the entire company of the greater and lesser cycles of the gods. Frequently the same god has different titles in different places; and the god of a certain town has generally a title given to him which shows that he inhabits that town, or is lord of it. The names of one god are at times very numerous, for example, in one inscription the Sun-god Rā is addressed under seventy-two different names, and a whole chapter of the Book of the Dead is given up to the

[1] The authorities to be consulted on this subject are Renouf, 'Hibbert Lectures;' Wilkinson, 'Ancient Egyptians,' 2nd edition, with Dr. Birch's notes; Brugsch, 'Religion und Mythologie der alten Aegypter, Part I., and Lanzone, 'Dizionaris di Mitologia Egizia,' Turin, 1881.

I

names of Osiris. In such lists we often find one god
identified with another, and indeed with several others ;
so then it is at once evident that a large number of the
minor deities are merely forms of the great gods ; and
the same statement applies even to the great gods themselves. For example, the god Rā when he rose in the
morning was called Harmachis, *i.e.*, Har on the horizon ;
at mid-day he was called Rā, and in the evening he was
Atum or Tmu. The gods were supposed to eat and drink,
and to have every attribute of man physical and mental.

The Egyptian word for god was *nutâr*, which word
Renouf considers to mean 'power.'   It has been ex-
plained by Brugsch as meaning the 'operative power
which engenders and makes things in a regular recurrence,
which endows them with new life, and gives back to
them their youthful freshness.' The Egyptian called
every god *nutâr ;* but in addition to this he seems to
have had an idea of God which will bear some comparison
in sublimity with our own.   For example, let us take an
extract from a hymn :—

God is One and Alone, and there is none other with Him.[1]
God is the One, the One who has made all things.[2]
God is a Spirit, a hidden Spirit, the Spirit of Spirits, the
    great Spirit of Egypt, the divine Spirit.[3]
God is from the beginning, and has existed from the
    beginning.[4]

Compare—
[1] Deut. vi. 4 ; 2 Sam. vii. 22; Is. xlv. 5, 21 ; Mal. ii. 10 ; 1 Cor. viii. 6 ;
Eph. iv. 6.   [2] John i. 3 ; Col. i. 16.
[3] John iv. 24 ; Heb. xii. 9.   [4] Gen. i. 1 ; John i. 1 ; Col. i. 17.

He is the primeval One, and existed when as yet nothing
existed : He existed when as yet there was nothing, and
whatever is, He made it after He was.[1]   He is the Father
of beginnings.[2]   God is Eternal,[3] He is everlasting, and
without end, Perpetual, Eternal : He has endured for
endless time, and will exist henceforward for ever.[4]

God is hidden, and no one hath perceived His form, no one
hath fathomed His likeness,[5] He is hidden in respect of
gods and men, and is a mystery to His creatures.[6]

God is the Truth,[7] He lives by Truth, He lives upon Truth,
He is the King of Truth.   .

God is Life, and man lives through Him alone.[8]

He blows the breath of Life[9] into their nostrils.

God is Father[10] and Mother ; the Father of fathers, and the
Mother of mothers.

God begets,[11] but he is not begotten, He gives birth to, but is
not given birth to.

He begets Himself, and gives birth to Himself, He makes,[12]
but is not made, He is the Creator of His own form,
and the Fashioner of His body.   God is the Creator

Compare—

[1] Rev. iv. 11.   [2] Rev. i. 8.   [3] Deut. xxxiii. 27 ; 1 Tim. i. 17.
[4] Ps. x. 16 ; xc. 2 ; cii. 25-27 ; Jer. x. 10.
[5] Ex. xxxiii. 20 ; John i. 18 ; 1 Tim. vi. 16.
[6] Job xxxvii. 23.
[7] Ps. xxv. 10 ; xxxi. 5 ; lvii. 3 ; lxxxix. 14 ; xci. 4 ; c. 5 ; cxlvi. 6 ;
Jer. x. 10 ; John xiv. 6.
[8] Acts xvii. 28.
[9] Gen. ii. 7 ; Job. xii. 10 ; xxxiii. 4 ; Ps. xxxiii. 6 ; Dan. v. 23 ; Acts
xvii. 25.
[10] Deut. xxxii. 6 ; Ps. xxvii. 10 ; lxviii. 5 ; Is. ix. 6 ; Mal. ii. 10.
[11] Ps. ii. 7 ; John i. 14, 18 ; iii. 16, 18 ; compare the 112th Surah of the
Koran.   [12] Prov. xvi. 4 ; Is. xlv. 12 ; Jer. xxvii. 5.

of heaven and earth, the deep, the water, and the mountains.   God stretches out the heavens, and makes firm the earth beneath.[1]

That which emanates from (*i.e.*, the desire of) His heart is performed immediately, and when He has once spoken, it actually comes to pass and endures for ever and ever.[2]

God is the father of the gods, and the progenitor of all deities.[3]

God is compassionate to those that fear Him[4] and hears those who cry unto Him.[5]   He protects the weak against the strong.[6]   God knows those who know Him,[7] He rewards those who serve Him,[8] and protects those who follow Him.[9]

In these sentences we see at once that the Egyptians had recognized the unity, eternity, and infinity of the Deity, as well as His loving-kindness.   Moreover, in the moral maxims laid down by the Egyptians it is very evident when they used the word God, they referred to a being with such attributes as have been stated above. As for example :—

To obey is to love God, but to disobey is to hate Him.[10]

Compare—

[1] Ps. civ. 5 ; Prov. viii. 28 ; Is. xl. 12 ; xlii. 5 ; Amos iv. 13.
[2] Ps. cxlviii. 5, 6.
[3] Deut. x. 17 ; Ps. lxxxvi. 8 ; cxxxv. 5.
[4] Ex. xxxiv. 6 ; Num. xiv. 18 ; 2 Chron. xiii. 9 ; Lam. iii. 22 ; Rom. ix. 15.
[5] Num. xx. 16 ; Ps. xxxiv. 17.
[6] Ps. xxxv. 10 ; Prov. xxii. 22, 23 ; Mal. iii. 5.
[7] Ps. i. 6 ; Nah. i. 7.
[8] Ps. lviii. 11 ; Is. xl. 10 ; Luke xix. 12–27.
[9] For the full German translation, see Brugsch, 'Religion und Mythologie,' p. 97.   [10] I Sam. xv. 22, 23.

Let not thy voice become loud in the temple of God, for
such things He abominates.[1]

God knows the wicked; He smites the wicked even to
blood.[2]

The most important of the Egyptian gods were :—

MALE.

Amen-Rā ...   .

Ptah ...   .

Harmachis ...   .

Rā ...   .

Mentu Rā ...   .

Seb ...   .

Osiris ...   .

Asar-hapi or Serapis ...   ...

Horus ...   .

Harpocrates ...   .

Bes ...   .

Anubis...   ...   .

Set ...   .

Compare—

[1] Eccles. v. 1, 2, 6 ; Matt. vi. 6, 7.

[2] Ps. lviii. 10 ; cxxix. 4 ; Prov. iii. 33 ; xiv. 11.

Thoth	...	...	...	
Shu	...	...	...	
Chnum	...	...	...	
Chonsu	...	...	...	
Tmu	...	...	...	
Sebak	...	...	...	

FEMALE.

Mut	...	...	...	
Seχet	...	...	...	
Bast	...	...	...	
Neith	...	...	...	
Nut	...	...	...	
Isis	...	...	...	
Athor	...	...	...	
Nephthys	...	...	...	
Ta-ur (Thoueris)	...	...	...	
Mā	...	...	...	
Hapi (the Nile)	...	...	...	

THE GENII OF THE DEAD.

Amset ...   .

Hapi ...   .

Tuaumutef   ...   .

Kebhsenuf   ...   .

THE ENEMY OF RĀ.

Apap ...   .

Ptah was the chief god, and was called the 'lord of truth.' He made the egg from which the sun and moon came forth, was the father of the gods, who came forth from his eye, and of men, who came forth from his mouth. His seat was Memphis, and he is represented as a mummy holding the symbols of life, stability and power, He was worshipped at Memphis under the form of Ptah-Socharis-Osiris, and under this form he was connected with Hades and the dead.

Sepulchral figures of Ptah-Socharis-Osiris are found with a box attached to them, to hold mummied objects. The animal sacred to Ptah was the Apis.

After Ptah came the great Sun-god Rā. He was the great god of Heliopolis, the 'city of the sun;' his father was Nu or the sky, across which he sailed in a boat His children were called Shu and Tefnut; and he waged war against the demon of darkness called Apap. In the morning the sun was called Harmachis

, at mid-day Rā, and at evening Tum. The Sun-god Rā died every night, but created himself anew each morning. The hawk and the Mnevis bulls were the animals sacred to him.

Osiris was the eldest child of Nut, 'the heaven,' and Seb,

Rā.

'the earth.' Before he was born he married his sister Isis, and they had a son called Horus. A brother and another sister of his, Set and Nephthys, also married each other. Osiris and Isis lived together very happily; but their brother Set conspired against him, and at a feast induced him to go into a box; it was immediately closed, carried to the Nile, thrown in, and borne away by the river. Isis, distracted with grief, searched everywhere for the

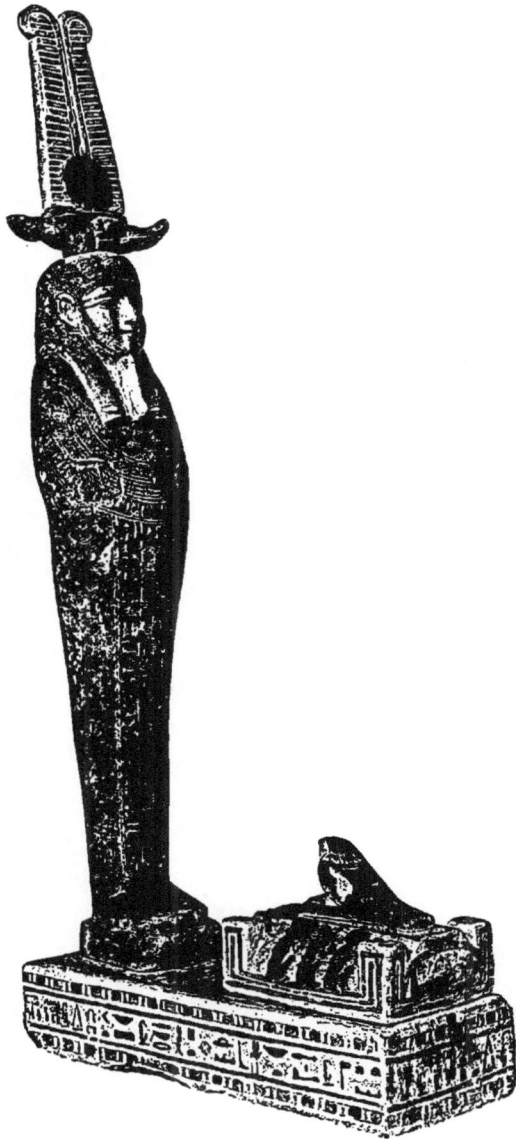

Figure of Ptah-Socharis-Osiris, and Box for holding Mummied Object.

body of her husband, and at last finding it she hid it, and went to fetch her son Horus, to help her to avenge his father. When out hunting one day, Set found the body of Osiris, cut it in pieces, and strewed them everywhere. The faithful Isis hearing this, gathered together the fragments and buried them ; and then she built a sepulchre over each. Osiris, however, still lived, and was king of the infernal regions. Now, the meaning of the story is this : Osiris and Isis are the offspring of the sky and the earth, Nut and Seb. Seb is represented as a goose 🦢, and, as such, laid the golden egg, the sun, or Osiris. Isis was the dawn, and Horus her son by Osiris was the sun in his full strength. The wicked brother and sister that conspired against Osiris were Set 𓊖, the Darkness, and Nephthys 𓎛, the Sunset. So the victory of Set over Osiris is the victory of night over day, or of darkness over light. On the following day Horus, or the sun in his strength, would arise and spread light over the whole world, and so his father Osiris would be revenged through his (Horus') victory over Set.

Osiris was called the ' good being,' and was the judge of the souls of the dead. In religious texts the deceased person is always called Osiris.

Anubis, the god of the dead, was the son of Nephthys and Osiris. He is called the ' Chief of the mountain,' i.e., of the western hills where the dead were buried. Anubis is represented in a picture as the embalmer of his father Osiris; and a common title of his was 'lord of embalming.'

The Egyptian god of writing and presiding deity of libraries was called Thoth, or in Egyptian Tahuti. He was the inventor of the arts, sciences, and astronomy, and he is usually represented ibis-headed. He was scribe in the infernal regions, and was supposed to keep

Thoth.

a record of the actions of the dead. In one hand he holds a palette, and with the other he traces with a reed the destiny of the deceased. He also represents the moon; and as a lunar god he wears either the disk of the full moon or the horns of the crescent moon upon his head. As the god of the moon he measured months, seasons, and years.

Tmu was another form of the Sun-god, and was the setting sun. He was considered to be the creator of men and things, and gave the 'cool breeze of the north wind' to mankind.

Nephthys ⌷, *neb ḥet*, 'the lady of the house,' was the wife of Set, the demon who fought against and conquered Osiris. She is represented on coffins and other sepulchral objects standing or kneeling at the bier of Osiris, and beating her head for grief at the death of her husband and brother.

Horus, or the 'young sun,' was the son of Osiris and the god who waged war with Set. He was the god called 'avenger of his father,' and his battles against darkness are the favourite theme of compositions in the later days of the Empire. The bird sacred to Horus was the hawk.

Mut, a goddess represented by a vulture, was one of the forms of the feminine creative principle.

Isis was the wife of Osiris, and had many forms. She gave life to and suckled the youthful Horus: hence a very large number of statues of this goddess represent her seated with Horus upon her knees and wearing a disk and horns upon her head.

Hathor or Athor is supposed to be a form of Isis. She is represented at times as a standing figure with a cow's head, upon which are a disk and horns; in her right hand she carries the symbol of life ☥, and in her left a sceptre ⌡. At other times she is depicted as a young and beautiful woman, with a vulture's head on her forehead, and wearing a disk and horns. Her name ⬚ *het Her*, means the 'house of Horus,' for it was supposed that he took refuge and grew up under the fostering care of this loving and protectful goddess.

Sekhet and Bast were the deities to whom the cat and lion were sacred. They are represented by standing figures having the head of a cat or lion, and wearing the disk of the sun and a uræus upon their head.

The god Chnumis was a form of the Sun-god. He is called the 'creator of mankind,' and is represented as having made man out of clay on a potter's wheel. He was also the original father of all the gods ; and when Osiris had been hacked to pieces by Set, he it was who reconstructed the body.

Amen-Rā, together with Mut and Chonsu, formed the great trinity at Thebes. Amen-Rā is represented as a man coloured blue, wearing two long feathers on his head, while in one hand he holds the symbol of life and in the other a sceptre. The word Amen means 'concealer,' and this god is often invoked as the 'concealer of his name.' He was a solar deity, and was styled 'lord of the thrones of the earth ;' and in him the attribute of every other deity was believed to be found.

The Egyptian was a firm believer in immortality, and it is not an uncommon thing to find the title '*living*' given to the deceased, indicating that his relatives considered him to be enjoying everlasting life.

During the festivals the gods were arrayed in sacred vestments, the colour and style of which were all prescribed by the sacred canons on this subject. The offerings to the gods consisted of incense, wine, oil, ointment, flowers, and sacred animals. The incense was made into small balls, and then thrown into a censer in the shape of a cup with a long handle. The sacrificing of sacred animals was a most important ceremony. Plutarch says that the most acceptable offering to the god was a red ox, which calls to mind the command to 'bring a red heifer without spot, wherein is no blemish, and upon which never came yoke.'[1] The law on this point was so strict, Plutarch says, that a single black or white hair rendered the beast unfit for sacrifice. With the Egyptians the heifer was sacred; and it is most probable that the Jews remembered this when they asked leave of Pharaoh to go a distance of three days in the wilderness to sacrifice to their God. The monuments, however, represent white and black oxen being sacrificed on the altars of the different gods, thereby showing that a red ox was not absolutely necessary for propitiating the gods. Among the offerings of plants the onion was a very favourite gift, and it seems to have been as great a favourite with the Egyptians as it was with the Hebrews. Ointment was presented in jars with the name of the deity for whom the ointment was intended inscribed upon it. When a king laden with rich booty returned from an

[1] Num. xix. 2.

expedition into foreign countries, the sanctuaries of the
gods were enriched with enormous gifts of untold value
as thanksgivings for the victory.   In the great Harris
Papyrus we are told that Rameses III. (among other
things) gave 10,047 cattle of different sorts, 73,800
cakes, 2,396 jars of dry dates, 4,339 waterfowl, 2,366
jars of onions, 41,980 living birds, 2,396 bottles of
grapes, 825,840 crystal beads, and 353,919 geese to the
temples of his land.

The priests of the gods formed the most important
caste in the land of Egypt.   A certain number of them
were always by the side of the king, and from this caste
Pharaoh always chose his ministers and judges.   They
offered sacrifices, and by their great knowledge they were
considered to be able to foresee coming events, and hence
to warn the king of the failure of an expedition, or to
foretell its success.   Dr. Birch considers the following to
be the principal orders of the priests :—[1]

	nutàr ḥen	prophet.
	nutàr àtf	divine father.
	àb	purifier.
	nutàr meri	'god beloved.'
	fa nutàr sentra	incense-bearer.
	ker ḥeb	prayer-reciter.
	ḥesi	bard or poet.

[1] Wilkinson's 'Ancient Egyptians,' i. p. 169.

Queens and women of high rank took part in the worship of the temples, and the principal dignities held by such were ⸗ nutâr hemt, or 'divine wife,' ⸗ nutâr tuat, ⸗ qema, and ⸗ ahi, 'sistrum-bearer.'

The most important order of the priests was that of 'prophet.' They were the authorities on every point connected with the worship of the gods and the ritual of the temple. The priests were most scrupulously clean in their habits and dress, and we are told that they bathed four times during the twenty-four hours, and shaved the whole body every three days. Their food was sufficient, but no more, and the utmost care was taken by them that nothing forbidden entered into it. They used wine sparingly, and in common with the Jews they hated the flesh of the pig, and were accustomed to eat mutton. All vegetables were not allowed to be eaten, but there can be no doubt that they enjoyed such things as were offered to the gods. In addition to their strict mode of life, they were compelled to study much, and to be skilled in all the sciences known in Egypt at that time. Their dress was usually made of linen, and very simple. The chief priest, however, wore a panther skin when he went to offer up sacrifice, or to take part in the different processions at a festival, and all the priests put on adornments during the service in the temples. In common with a large

K

number of the people, they practised the rite of
circumcision, and this was considered a distinctive mark
between the Egyptians and the barbarians.

The power of the priests in Egypt must have been
enormous, for not only did they belong socially to the
highest caste in the land, but by their knowledge of
profane sciences and their direction of the ceremonies and
worship of the gods, whose representatives they were, they
acquired such a power and hold over the king and people,
that it would be exceedingly difficult to perform anything
of national importance without their aid.   Moreover, the
right understanding of the beliefs and dogmas of the
religion of the land was locked up in their breasts, and
the knowledge of the mysteries of the gods was their
peculiar property.   Little by little, too, everything connected with the administration of the land fell under
the directing influence of their authority.   They took
a very prominent part in the processions of the gods,
and a certain number of them carried the arks of their
gods in the festivals.   Festivals were very frequent in
Egypt, and the mere enumeration of the most important
of them takes up several lines on the sepulchral tablets.

The Egyptian's belief in the immortality of the soul,
and matters of a kindred nature, we shall consider in
the chapter relating to the mummy.

CHAPTER VII.

THE BURIAL OF THE DEAD.

THE most casual observer, on examining the Egyptian collection of any of our European museums, will be at once struck with surprise on seeing how large a portion of it relates to the sepulchre and funereal rites of an Egyptian. The most splendid objects, the best workmanship, and the costliest things, were dedicated to the tomb of the deceased by the loving relatives. It will be readily understood that all tombs were not equally beautiful, for then as now the magnificence of a funeral depended upon the will and the power of the relatives to pay for it ; but apparently every one did his best to make the tomb of his friend or beloved as magnificent as his circumstances permitted.

The making of tombs, as well as their decoration, appears to have been carried out by one of the grades of the priests, who no doubt persuaded those who could afford it to indulge in a splendid funeral, for this not only tended to their own magnificence, but to their profit. And it is very certain that only the wealthy could afford to indulge in the luxury of a tomb, with its chambers and costly decorations of rows of hieroglyphs and vignettes : also the cost of the coffins and the process of mummifying would be considerable. The

tombs themselves belonged to the priests, who apparently kept several in readiness for the family of the
deceased to choose from.   Inscriptions and chapters of
the Book of the Dead and other sacred books were
inscribed also upon its walls, as well as pictures which
represented the life of an ordinary mortal, so that the
series would apply equally well to the life of any

Female Mourners for the Dead.

purchaser; the only part left blank in the text being
places in which the names of the deceased and his titles
could be filled in.   We have copies of the Book of the
Dead in which the name of the deceased is wanting
entirely, the reason being that the friends of the dead
man went in a hurry to the place where inscribed papyri
could be bought, and finding one 'ready made' which
suited their purse, they buried it with him, not taking

the trouble to have his name inserted in the places where it should be.

The friends of the dead of all classes endeavoured to bury a copy of the whole or part of the Book of the Dead with their beloved, for it was considered of the greatest importance that the deceased in his journey and wanderings through the nether world should possess the mystic power imparted by the magic words, formulæ, and prayers of the book, which was supposed to be of divine origin, having been written by no less a deity than Thoth, the recorder of the destinies of mankind. The greatest frauds were perpetrated in this way, for the scribe, knowing that in all probability the papyrus would never be unrolled, would not take the pains, if he were lazy, to write carefully and well, or if he were ignorant would make hundreds of mistakes; while if he were both ignorant *and* lazy, he would produce such hopeless confusion in an inscription that not even the most learned scribe or priest could make sense of it. Again, if the scribe were ever so well disposed, but had to copy from a hieratic version, and did not understand what he was writing, he would undoubtedly make scores of blunders.

When an important person needed a tomb, the purchase was usually effected by means of a legal document; but if a man died in debt the tomb was seized by the creditors, who could even prevent the deceased from being buried therein. Diodorus tells us that the Egyptians called their houses hostelries, on

account of the short time which they dwelt in them;
but they called the tombs 'eternal dwelling-places.'
This latter statement is fully borne out by the
inscriptions, for they call the tomb 'house of everlasting.'[1]

From investigations made by Mariette at Sakkarah,
it appears that a tomb, or *mastaba*, of the ancient
Empire consisted of a chamber or series of chamber
above ground, a narrower chamber or corridor, and
a deep pit sunk into the rock, which led to a vault
for holding the sarcophagus. When a visitor entered
the chamber and looked around, he saw the walls
(frequently covered with pictures), and a stele facing to
the east, which was always covered with a hieroglyphic
inscription. This chamber was always found without a
door, and the stele with the inscription appears to have
been the most important part of the chamber; while in
the corridor next to the chamber were placed images or
statues of the deceased. Often this part of the tomb
had no communication whatever with the other parts of
it, for it was walled up entirely and for ever: at other
times a small square opening was made in it, in order to
allow the perfume of the incense offered in the other
chamber to come in to the statues. The pit or well was
square, and varied in depth from 40 to 80 feet; there
was neither staircase nor ladder leading from the upper
part of the tomb to the bottom of the pit, and unless

[1] , *pa t'et.*

provided with a rope ladder, it was impossible for a visitor to descend. Following a narrow passage leading from the pit, the sarcophagus chamber was reached, in one corner of which stood the sarcophagus itself. How difficult it was to break into a tomb to do harm to the mummy is at once seen, since it would be necessary to obtain entrance to the chamber or chapel, to break through the partition wall separating the chamber from the corridor, and to find means of descent into the pit itself.

Let us go back again to the first chamber. Within the chamber, and over the door of the tomb, the same inscription was carved, which prayed: 'May Anubis, who dwells within the divine house, grant a royal oblation. May sepulture be granted in the nether world, in the land of the divine Menti, the ancient, the good, the great, to him (*i.e.*, the departed) who is faithful to the great god. May he advance upon the blissful paths upon which those advance who are faithful to the great god. May the funereal oblations be paid to him at the beginning of the year, on the feast of Tehuti, on the first day of the year, on the feast of Uaka, on the feasts of the Great and of the Small Heat, on the apparition of Sechem at the feast of Uaka, at the feasts of each month, and the half-month, and every day.'[1] Other prayers ask that the god will ensure the gift of funereal offerings to the deceased,

---

[1] Renouf, 'Hibbert Lectures,' p. 131 ; 'Revue Archéologique,' p. 82, vol. xix., 1869.

and that he will cause him to be buried after a 'happy old age.'

But the tomb, besides serving for the abode of the dead, was also the page upon which the biography of its builder was written.   The rich and wealthy Egyptian first chose out his place of sepulture, and when all its parts were built under his own superintendence, he caused the principal passages of his life to be drawn in vivid colours upon the walls of the upper chamber.   He was depicted leading a life of luxury, he hunted, he fished, he made expeditions, he was surrounded by a large retinue of servants, and nothing of importance was omitted from these illustrations of his life.   At times the builder did not live to finish his tomb, hence Mariette found at Sakkarah a number of incomplete tombs; and he mentions a curious case where a tomb was built for one Ape-em-ankh, but in the corridor two inscriptions are found stating that he gave up his own tomb to his wife and to his son, who died very young.

But how were the poor buried?   Judging from the skeletons which remain, they were simply buried in the sand to the depth of about a yard; for traces of neither coffins nor bandages have been found.   In the latter days of the Egyptian empire, stelæ which were erected by the friends or family of the deceased often contain a summary of his life, his titles and various offices, his good works, and he is made to speak and proclaim his good deeds.   The following translation will illustrate this custom.

STELE OF NEXT-AMES.

1. Dated the 1st day of the . . . . . . month of the spring of the . . . . . . year of the Majesty of Her Rā, the powerful bull, the saffron diademed, the lord of the two crowns, the supremely mighty, the destroyer of the Asiatics, the golden hawk, the creator of the two earths ;

2. king of the north and south, chief of the nine bows, Rā-χeperu-ari-māt, son of the Sun of his belly, lord of diadems, godly father Ai, god, ruler of Uast, Osiris, lord of Abydos beloved, giving life.

3. May . . . . south and north, and Anubis upon his hill grant to me glory in heaven, power upon earth, and triumph in χer-neter.[1] May they grant that I go in and come forth from my tomb,

4. that my majesty refresh its shade, that I drink water from my own cistern every day, that all my limbs be solid, that the Nile

5. give me bread and flowers of every kind at the season, that I pass over the length of my land every day without ceasing, and that my soul

6. may light upon the branches of the trees which I have planted. May I refresh my face beneath my sycamores, may I eat bread of their giving,

7. may I have my mouth wherewith I may speak like the followers of Horus, may I come forth to heaven, may I descend to earth, may I be not shut out upon

8. the road, may there not be done to me what my *ka* execrates, may my soul never be captive, may I be in the midst of the obedient, among the faithful.

[1] Or Hades.

9. May I plough my fields in Seχet-Aaru, may I attain the
'Field of Peace,' may one come out to me with jugs of
beer and cakes,

10. the cakes of the lords of eternity, may I receive my slice
from the joint upon the table of the great god; I the
ka of Neχt-Ames, first prophet of the god Ames.

11. He says : I have done the behests of men and the will of
the gods, wherefore I have given bread to the hungry,
and I have satisfied the indigent.   I have followed

12. the god in his temple, my mouth hath not spoken
insolently against my superior officers, there hath been
no haughtiness in my step, but I have walked
measuredly (*gradatim*), I have performed the law
beloved by the king.

13. I understood his commands, in my place I watched to
exalt his will, I rose up for his worship every day, I
gave my mind to what

14. he said without ever hesitating at what he determined
with reference to me, I took uprightness and fairness,
I understood the things about which I should keep
silence.

15. The lord my king refreshed and favoured me for my well
doing, he saw that my hands were vigorous through my
heart, he advanced my seat exceedingly, he placed me
in the council chamber, me,

16. the *ka* of Neχt-Ames, triumphant, the superintendent of
the prophets of the lords of Apu.   Says he : O ye
living upon earth, living for eternity, enduring for ever,
ye priests

17. and ministrants of Osiris, everyone learned in divine
traditions; when ye enter my sepulchre and pass

through it, do ye utter your prayers by my tablet and
do ye proclaim my name without cessation in

18. the presence of the lords of law.   So may your gods
favour you, and may ye transfer your dignities to your
children after a full old age, provided that ye say,

19. 'May Osiris grant a royal oblation to Neχt-Ames, lord of
fidelity, superintendent of works in the temple of Ai,
prince and first prophet of Ames and Isis.   May his
memorial abide in the seat of eternity.'[1]

[1] 'Trans. Soc. Bib. Arch,' vol. viii., Part III., p. 298.

CHAPTER VIII.

The Mummy.

THE ancient Egyptians are the only people known
who have succeeded in bringing the art of embalming or
mummifying to perfection. They believed that the

Soul with Symbols of Life and Breath revisiting Mummied Body.

soul would revisit the body after a number of years, and
therefore it was absolutely necessary that the body
should be preserved, if its owner wished to live for ever

with the gods. This belief appears to be very old, and allusion is made to it in the Book of the Dead. The Egyptians attributed to man a *soul*, which they represented as a hawk with a human head [symbol] a *ka* [symbol] or *image,* and a *shadow* [symbol]; this last was given back to him in his second life. The *ka* or image is the being to whom funereal gifts were made. It must not for a moment be imagined that the Egyptians worshipped the statues of the deceased, for it was the living *ka* which was supposed to reside in the stone or wood that was the object of adoration. The *ka* was not an attribute peculiar to man, for every god had one, and in one place we are told that the god Rā has seven souls and fourteen *kau* (plural of *ka*). The soul, however, had its own body, and was supposed to be able to eat and to drink.[1] The soul was an emanation from the god of the universe, and after it left the body it was doomed to undergo a series of existences, until it arrived at a fit state of purity to be absorbed into its original counterpart.

The Greek historians mention three ways in which mummies were made. In the first, the brain was extracted through the nose, and the intestines were

---

[1] The whole of this subject is exceedingly difficult : the reader is referred to Mr. Le Page Renouf's article on the Ka, in ' Trans. Soc. Bib. Arch.,' vi. p. 405 ; and to M. Maspero's monograph on this matter. Also for a discussion on the Soul and the Shade, see Dr. Birch's paper in ' Trans. Soc. Bib. Arch.,' viii. pt. III. ; and Mr. W. H. Rylands, F.S.A., has drawn many scenes from the monuments illustrating this subject.

removed.   The body was then filled with myrrh, cassia,
etc., after which it was steeped in natron for seventy
days.   After the seventy days were over, the body was
washed and swathed in linen bandages gummed on the
inside until every part of it was covered.   In the second,
a material, called oil of cedar, was introduced, which
dissolved the intestines, so that they could be removed
without mutilating the body.   It was then laid in natron,
which dissolved the greater part of the flesh, and left
only the skin and bones.   In the third, the body was
merely salted for seventy days, and then given back to
the friends.   The first method would cost about £250
of our money, the second £60, while the third would
be very cheap.

An examination of the mummies shows that many
different processes of embalming were in use at different
periods in Egypt ; and that the Egyptians possessed
a good knowledge of the use of medicines and anatomy.
The intestines that were taken out of the body were
dedicated to the four genii of the Amenti or Hades,
whose names were Amset, Hapi, Tuaumutef, and
Kebhsenuf.   To the first were dedicated the larger
intestines, to the second the smaller intestines, to the
third the heart, and to the fourth the liver.   These were
placed in four jars, which had covers made in the shape
of a man, an ape, a jackal, and hawk respectively.
These jars were placed in the tomb with the sarcophagus,
and in the pictures which are painted on the outside of
mummies, these are often seen standing beneath the bier.

Mummy of the lady Katebt, a Musician of the God Amen, from Thebes.
Now in the British Museum.

When the friends of a poor person wished his intestines to be under the protection of these genii, and could not afford to go to the expense of alabaster or wooden jars, they caused four waxen figures of these gods to be made, and placed inside the body with the intestines.

When the body had been mummified, and wrapped up in linen bandages, it was a common thing, if the deceased was a person of rank or a priest, to enclose it in what is called a *cartonnage*. The cartonnage was a thin casing made of plaster and linen, and it covered the whole body, fitting closely. In the earlier days the face was painted only, but in the time of the Ptolemies the face and ears were often gilded, and the eyes, eyebrows and lids made of glass or porcelain. On the top of the head a scarabæus or beetle was painted holding the sun between its *antennæ*, while at the foot was painted a figure of Nut or heaven, overshadowing the mummy, and Isis and Nephthys, the wife and sister of the Osiris or mummy, stand one on each side of it, with wings stretched out to protect the deceased. At one time the mummy of the deceased is represented as being visited by his soul, or with the sun shining upon him, and at another the judgment scene from the one hundred and twenty-fifth chapter of the Book of the Dead is shown, with the soul of the deceased being weighed in the balance before Osiris, the great god of the dead, while the four genii of the dead look on. The scenes depicted on the cartonnages vary, very few being exactly alike. On some mummies scarabæi, necklaces, rows of beads,

L

breastplates, and figures are found ; and at times objects
which were used by the deceased in life have been buried
with him, as in the case of the sacred bard Anχ-hapi,
whose cymbals were found with his mummy, and may
be seen in the British Museum.   In the last days of the
Egyptian empire a portrait of the deceased was painted
and laid upon the face of the mummy ; and over the
mummy of a child in the British Museum there is a
covering on which is painted the face and figure of the
little Greek.   The hair was mummified, and wrapped in
bandages and laid at the foot of the mummy.

The mummy being arranged in its gaudily painted
cartonnage, was then placed in a coffin or case of
sycamore wood, which was usually made to represent
the form of a man.   As the mummy, so the coffin was
made according to the amount of money the friends of
the deceased could afford to pay.   The rich indulged
in most beautiful coffins, covered inside and out with
scenes and chapters from the Book of the Dead,
allegorical representations, etc., while in the later days
under the Ptolemies, zodiacs are often found.   The
outer case of all was made of stone, and was sometimes
covered entirely with hieroglyphs, and at other times
various scenes were introduced to illustrate the text.
The magnificent stone sarcophagus of Hor-em-heb in
the British Museum is inscribed with a series of pictures
representing the passage of the sun through the hours
of the day, and above each scene are lines of hieroglyphs
saying what gods are portrayed, and what is meant by

the pictures. The scarabæi which were deposited with the mummy were made of various substances, and were usually inscribed with the thirtieth chapter of the Book of the Dead, which has for its vignette the deceased

Scarabæus inscribed with a part of the Thirtieth Chapter of the Ritual of the Dead.

adoring a scarabæus, and whose rubric directs that this chapter should be 'said over a scarabæus of hard stone. Cause it to be washed with gold, and placed within the heart of a person. Make a phylactery anointed with oil,

say over it with magic: My heart is my mother, my
heart is my transformations.'[1]

The figures placed with the dead were called *ushabtiu*,
and were inscribed with the name of the deceased and
the sixth chapter of the Book of the Dead.   They were
supposed to do for the deceased in Hades all the work
that would otherwise fall to his lot, such as the ploughing
of fields and drawing water.

Besides   men   and   women,   the   Egyptians   also
mummified cats, crocodiles, snakes, birds such as the
ibis and hawk, and many other creatures.

[1] Dr. Birch, in Bunsen's ' Egypt,' v. 139.

Ushabti Figures containing the Sixth Chapter of the Ritual of the Dead.

CHAPTER IX.

THE BOOK OF THE DEAD.

THIS is the name usually given by Egyptologists to a book or collection of chapters which the Egyptians called 'coming forth by day.' There are a very large number of copies of this book in the various museums of Europe, and parts of it are inscribed upon papyrus, tombs, coffins, mummies, *ushabtiu* figures, scarabæi, and other objects. In many copies the chapters are accompanied by vignettes, but the arrangement of the chapters is never the same in any two manuscripts, and many of the hieroglyphic copies upon papyrus show that they have been copied from the hieratic character, for the scribe has confused signs which are alike in that style of writing. The work in some form is exceedingly old, for there are evidences as far back as the eleventh dynasty that the knowledge of the meaning of certain parts of it had been already lost. As it is now, it is by no means easy to understand, on account of the allusions to legends in it, and its writer or writers imagining that the reader understands the whole system of religion and mythology. The first complete copy of the text was published by Lepsius in 1842 ; and in 1867 Dr. Birch published a literal translation of it in Bunsen's 'Egypt's Place in Universal History,' Vol. V.

From the Book of the Dead we gather that the religious man gained everlasting life ; first living in Hades as he lived upon earth, then passing through whatever transformations he wished, and finally being identified with Osiris, the god of the dead.   The rubric of the first chapter says : ' Let this book be known on earth.   It is made in writing on the coffin.   It is the chapter by which he comes out every day as he wishes, and he goes to his house.   He is not turned back.   There are given to him food and drink, slices of flesh off the altar of the Sun.   When he passes from the fields of the Elysium, corn and barley are given to him out of them.   For he is supplied as he was on earth.'[1]

In the accompanying illustration the future state of the blessed dead is depicted.   The outer border is the waters of the Nile.   In the top left-hand corner of the scene are three lakes, underneath which is the inscription : ' Being in peace in the fields of the Seχet-Aaru.'   Before the 'gods of the horizon' is a table laden with offerings, and a hawk called ' Peace, the Great Lord of Heaven.' The deceased is seen offering to the soul, and he paddles along in a boat containing tables of offerings.   Behind the boat is the ' cycle of the great gods,' to whom the deceased offers : and last of all comes Thoth, writing on a palette.   In the second division, the deceased is offering to Hapi or the Nile, and is represented performing all

[1] Bunsen, ' Egypt,' v. p. 163.

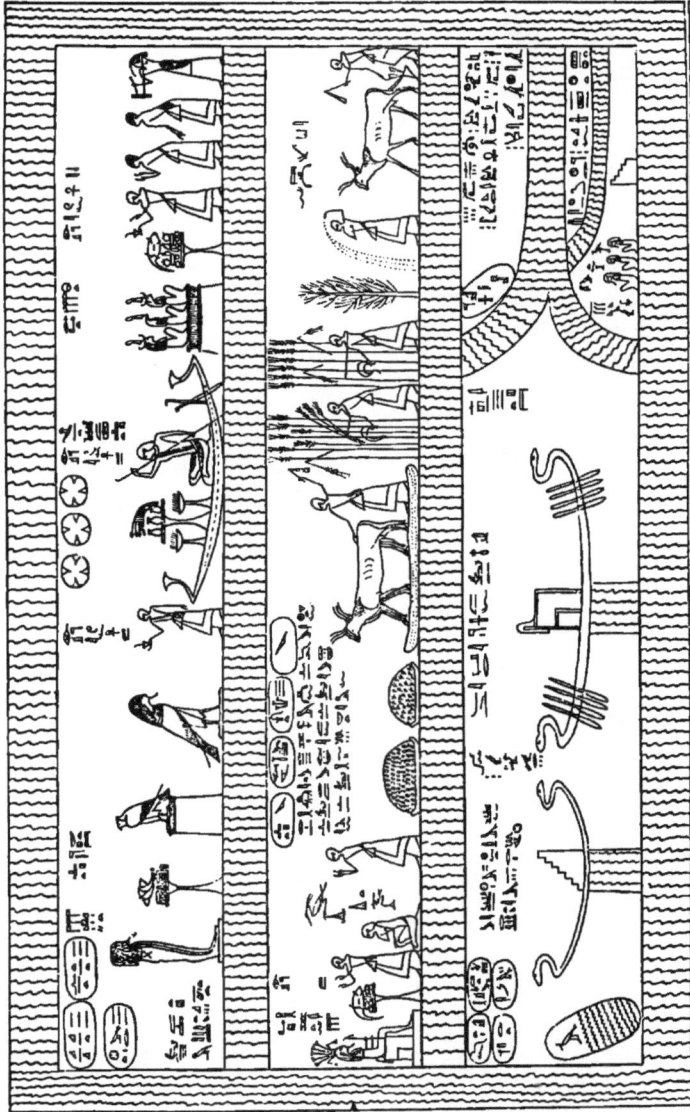

The Elysian Fields. *From Lepsius' 'Todtenbuch.'*

the various labours of the field, ploughing, sowing, and reaping. In the third division are four pools, and the

Part of the Seventeenth Chapter of the Ritual of the Dead. The Deceased in a Hall; the Boat of the Ram rowed by the Kings.

boat of Rā Harmachis, 'when he travels to the fields of the Seχet-Aaru.' Next comes the boat of Un-nefer or Osiris, with paddles and a throne. This division is

intersected by smaller streams of water: in the upper
part, or 'abode of the beatified dead,' dwells the Sun-
god, and there the corn grows to the height of seven
cubits; the lower part.is the dwelling-place of the gods,
and the gods represented are Shu, Tefnut, and Seb.

The seventeenth chapter of the Book of the Dead is
very important, as it contains explanations of what is
laid down therein in a series of questions and answers;
for example :—

> I am that splendid Bird *Bennu*, which is in Heliopolis.
> What does this mean?
> The *Bennu* bird is Osiris who is in Heliopolis.
> I have set two feathers upon my head.
> What do these two feathers signify?
> The two feathers are the two uræi crowns upon the head of
> my father Tum.

The transformations of the blessed dead could be as
numerous as they pleased, and a number of chapters
in the Book of the Dead are taken up in discussing them.
The progress of the soul in the nether world was barred by
countless demons, who waited to seize and destroy it : but
their power was utterly shattered if the deceased knew
certain words which were to be uttered. Attacks were
made upon all parts of the body, especially the heart ;
hence we find that several chapters are devoted to the
purpose of teaching how these may be warded off or
rendered powerless. Even after all danger from the
attack of devils was over for the deceased, there still

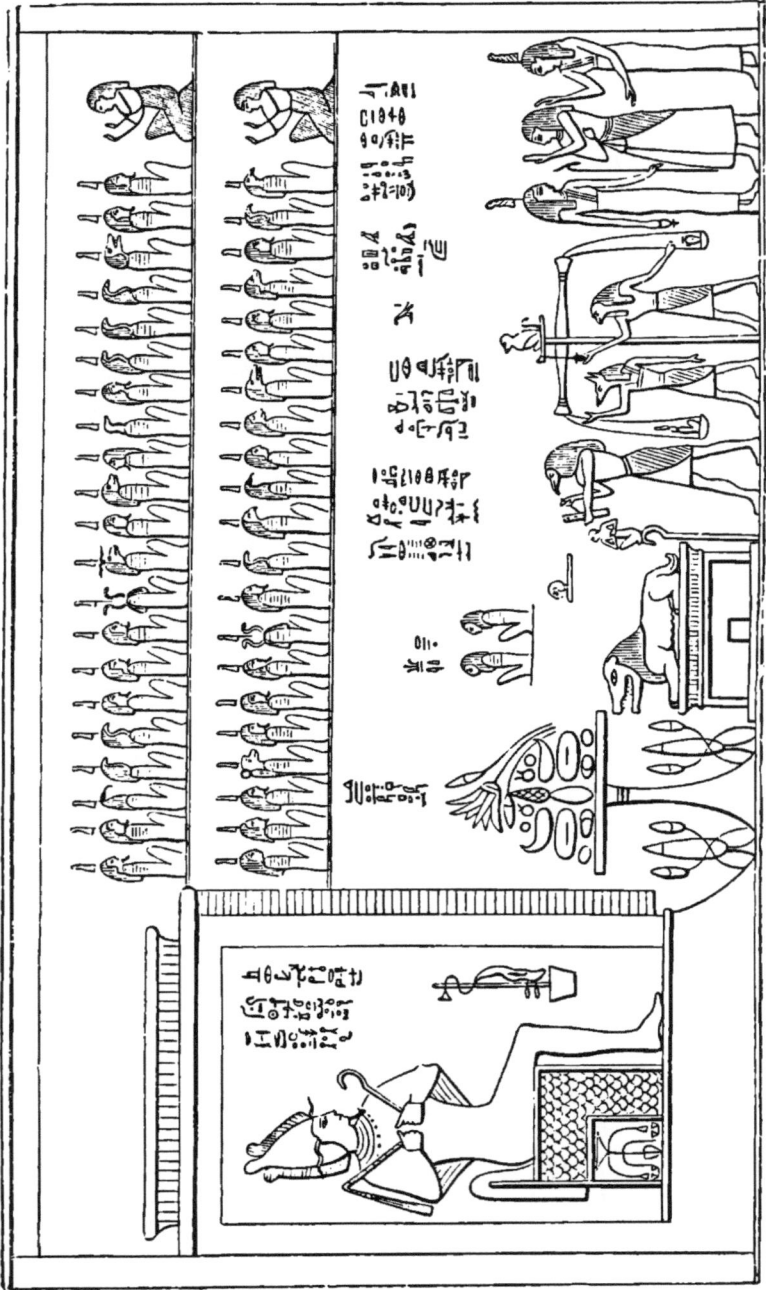

The Judgment Hall of Osiris.

remained the great and final judgment, which took place
before Osiris and the forty-two judges of the dead
in the Hall of the Two Truths. In the accompanying
illustration Osiris is sitting on a throne, and holding the
whip and sceptre indicative of royalty and dominion.
In front of him is an inscription which reads: ' Osiris,
the Good Being, the lord of life, the great god and ruler
within Rustat and Akart, Khent Amenti, the great god,
lord of Abydos, the king everlasting.' The forty-two
figures are the judges of the dead, each of whom bore a
name descriptive of his part. Before the hall of Osiris
is a table laden with offerings, and above it are the
four genii of the dead, Amset, Hapi, Tuaumutef, and
Kebhsenuf. Near the table is the destroyer of enemies,
a composite monster, and behind him stands Thoth,
writing the decision on a palette; while his cynoce-
phalus companion is seated on the middle of the
balance. The heart of the deceased is being weighed
in the right-hand pan of the scale against righteousness
in the other. Horus has his arm stretched out to the
indicator of the balance, and Anubis is watching the
pan of the scale in which the figure of Māt, righteousness, is seated. On the other side of the heart stand
two figures of the goddess of right or law, holding a
sceptre, and between them is the deceased. The deceased
then makes what is called the ' negative confession,' that
is a confession in which he declares to each god that he
has not committed a particular sin or crime, thus :—

Oh Strider, coming out of Heliopolis! I have not been idle.

Oh Gaper, coming out of Kar! I have not waylaid.

Oh Nostril, coming out of Hermopolis! I have not boasted.

Oh Devourer of Shades, coming out of the orbits! I have not stolen.

Oh Foul one, coming out of Rusta! I have not smitten men privily.

Oh Smoking Face, coming out after entering Heliopolis! I have not stolen the things of the Gods.

Oh Cracker of Bones, coming out of Bubastis! I have not told falsehoods.

Oh Glowing Feet, coming out of the Darkness! I have not eaten the heart.

Oh Eater of Blood, coming from the Block! I have not killed sacred beasts.

Oh Ruler of the Dead, coming out of the cave! I have not corrupted women or men.

Oh Swallower, coming out of Khenem! I have not blasphemed.

Oh Lord of Purity, coming out of Sais! I have not multiplied words in speaking.

Oh Nefer Tmu, coming out of Ptah-ka! I have not lied or done any wicked sin.

Oh Eye in his Heart, coming out of Sahu! I have not defiled the river.

Oh Yoker of Good, coming out of Heliopolis! I have not injured the Gods, or calumniated the slave to his master.[1]

---

[1] Bunsen's 'Egypt,' v. p. 254.

In the early part of the one hundred and twenty-fifth chapter the deceased says :—

Hail, ye Gods who are in the Hall of Truth without any deceit in your bodies, living off the dead in Heliopolis, devouring their hearts before Horus in his disk ! Save ye me from the god who feeds off the chief vitals on the day of the great judgment. Let the Osiris go ; ye know he is without fault, without evil, without sin, without crimes. Do not torture, do not anything against him. He lives off truth, he has made his delight in doing what men say, and the gods wish. The god has welcomed him as he has wished. He has given food to the hungry, drink to the thirsty, clothes to the naked, he has made a boat for me to go by. He has made the sacred food of the Gods, the meals of the Spirits. Take ye them to him, guard ye them for him. Therefore do not accuse him before the Lord of the Mummies; because his mouth is pure, his hands are pure.

Further on comes a list of the offences which the deceased has not committed, some of them being identical with those mentioned above.

If the deceased succeeds in passing this ordeal satisfactorily, he comes forth at once as a god (there is no place of probation), he becomes identified with Osiris, in whose shape his mummy was made, and he roams through the fields of bliss at pleasure. The whole family of Osiris then do for him as they have done for the god himself, all his enemies are slain, their necks and legs are broken, and they are annihilated for ever. In future nothing can do him harm, and if all the legions

M

of night and darkness conspire to hurt them, their efforts are powerless, for he is a 'GREAT GOD.' When the deceased has thus triumphed, his soul, his *ka*, and his shadow are all restored to him, and they are never more to be separated.

The Egyptian was a fatalist, he believed in dreams, ghosts, and demoniacal possession, yet his high moral ideal as exhibited by the inscriptions was of the purest and best; and when we compare his lofty conceptions of the Deity with those of other nations, we see that he stands remarkably alone. Thousands of years before Christ, he had arrived at these ideas, and it will be readily imagined that such a sensible and thoughtful man was not so utterly ridiculous in his religious views as he has been made to appear. Much that was absurd, such as the belief in magical words, charms, and names, had crept into his religion; but it is quite impossible to believe that the learned priests did not perceive its futility, even though they did not oppose it actively. Still, underneath the heap of rubbish which gathered round their religion, there lie grains of truth and lofty morality which are worth picking up even by the civilised nations of to-day.

CHAPTER X.

THE LIFE OF THE ANCIENT EGYPTIANS.

THE 'manners and customs' of the ancient Egyptians are made known to us by the histories of Herodotus, Diodorus Siculus and others, and by the pictures on the monuments and papyri.[1]

When a child was born in Egypt, the mother made an offering to the local divinity. The rearing of the child of poor parents cost very little, for their food was very simple, and their dress scanty and cheap; frequently they wore nothing at all, not even sandals. The children of rich or well-to-do parents would have an abundance of toys and playthings, and would be dressed in the richest stuffs. The toys consisted of dolls, figures of animals, and the like: the British Museum possesses several specimens, and has recently acquired a curious example of a toy in the shape of a wooden cat with inlaid glass eyes, and a movable lower jaw well lined with teeth. The mother carried her child in a shawl tied round her. The children were educated

---

[1] For fuller information as to the life of the Egyptians, the reader is referred to the excellent work of Sir Gardner Wilkinson, ' The Manners and Customs of the Ancient Egyptians,' 2nd edition.

according to their station and their future position in
life. They were kept in strict subjection by their
parents, and respect to old age was particularly in-
culcated ; the children of the priests were educated very
thoroughly in writing of all kinds, hieroglyphic, hieratic,
and demotic, and in the sciences of astronomy, mathe·
matics, etc. The Jewish deliverer Moses was educated
after the manner of the priests, and the 'wisdom of the
Egyptians' became a proverbial expression among the
outside nations, as indicating the utmost limit of human
knowledge.

Women of rank wore a skirt made of rich stuff
fastened at the waist, and over their shoulders a large
loose robe, which was tied at the waist. They wore
costly head-dresses, and their hair was usually plaited.
Long hair was considered beautiful, and packets of hair
are found with mummies, showing how much it was
prized. In the later days of the empire they wore
earrings, generally made of gold ; and the custom of
wearing rings on the fingers was common and wide-
spread. The necklace was a very favourite ornament
with both sexes, and the reader will get a very good
idea of its varieties by a few minutes' study of those
exhibited in the first Egyptian room of the British
Museum. Two very important articles of an Egyptian
lady's toilet were the *kohl* pot, and the ointment vase. The
former contained a substance, frequently antimony,
with which the ladies were accustomed to paint a black
line round their eyes, to make them appear larger, and

so increase their beauty. The Bible reader will not
need to be reminded that Jezebel painted her eyes when
she heard that Jehu was coming to Jezreel;[1] and this
custom is referred to elsewhere in Scripture.[2] The
kohl was applied to the eyes by means of a little stick,
thick at one end ; the British Museum possesses a large
number of *kohl* pots, some pierced with as many as
five holes, in which the various unguents of an Egyptian
lady's toilet were kept. The Egyptian lady used a
copper mirror, very highly polished ; the handles were
of different shapes, and frequently bore the name of the
owner. Baths with the Egyptians, as with the Romans,
were considered of primary importance.

The Egyptian gentleman wore a kind of apron, and a
sleeved garment, which he fastened round his waist with
a girdle or sash like the women. The dress of the
priests and the sacred scribes was made of linen, but in
other respects resembled that of an ordinary gentleman.
The men always shaved, but locks of hair were left on
certain parts of the heads of children. The dress of the
king was most gorgeous, consisting of robes of the most
beautiful stuffs and the richest ornaments. His head-
dress was a short wig, to the front of which was attached
a serpent. Both sexes wore sandals, made of a sort of
wicker work or leather ; they were sometimes carried
by attendants, and were always taken off in the presence
of the king.

The monuments give us no information about the

---

[1] 2 Kings ix. 30.   [2] Jer. iv. 30 ; Ezek. xxiii. 40.

marriage ceremony, but it appears that if a man married a second wife while the first was living, he was compelled to pay a heavy fine to the first wife, and her son inherited the property.   Polygamy was certainly practised by some of the nobles and kings of Egypt ; but as a rule the monuments give us the idea that the Egyptians were very affectionate in their domestic relations, and so the peace of the house was not likely to be broken by the introduction of a second wife.   The kings sometimes married foreigners, for Rameses II. took a daughter of the prince of the Khita to wife.   The Egyptian priests, like the Jewish, were allowed to have one wife only.   The wife was reckoned in genealogies, and a woman was not forbidden by law to rule over the kingdom.   The marriage of brother and sister was a custom that obtained, and the Ptolemies are notorious examples of this practice.

The king, as being the representative of the god Rā upon earth, was the highest and most important man in Egypt.   It was necessary that he should be a learned man, a warrior, and able to rule.   He bore various titles of honour, 'son of the Sun' being not the least among them.   Royal names were enclosed in a *cartouche* ⬭, and each king had a different appellation, which was placed before the family name, and is generally called the prenomen.   The king declared war and made peace, he was the god and father of the land, he judged cases in public, and in war he led the army. He took part in the processions of offerings to the gods,

and was priest as well as king; he made offerings
to the gods personally, entreating them to give him a
prosperous and happy reign. The Egyptian king, like
the Jewish, was anointed, and his double crown was
supposed to be given him by his favourite deities. In
one scene Rameses II. is being crowned by Set, above
whose head is written, 'I set up thy head-dress on thy
head like thy father Amen-Ra;'[1] and on the other side
of the king stands Thoth, holding a palm branch
plentifully notched, indicative of a long number of years,
while above him is written, 'I give thee duration of life
of years like Tmu.'

The dignity of king was hereditary, but queens were
allowed to rule when the lawful heir was too young.
The first object of the king was supposed to be the
welfare of his people, both temporal and spiritual.
Minor matters of administration would be disposed of
by his subordinates, but things of importance would
come before him and be discussed with his leading
advisers and councillors. When the king died, or
ascended to heaven, as the Egyptians would say, the
son of the Sun was dead, and hence universal mourning
prevailed in the land. The temple services ceased, the
whole of the business arrangements of the towns were
unhinged, and a general fast was observed; and just as
the king during life surpassed every one else by his
glory, so in death the beauty of his funeral and its
appointments surpassed that of all others. The greatest

[1] Wilkinson, iii. p. 361.

care was taken of the mummies of the great kings, and the safest spots were chosen in the mountains and elsewhere for their places of burial. The mummy was taken by a procession which crossed the river in boats, and then wended its way to the west of Thebes, Memphis, or wherever the tombs were. It was then lifted from the bier, and placed upright in the tomb, and ceremonies were performed before it by the priest or priests. The great cemetery, or 'land of life' as the Egyptians called it, was at Memphis, where the remains of thousands upon thousands of people have been found, for it was the burial-place of that region for thousands of years.

The Egyptians lived in houses which consisted generally of two stories, built for the most part of unbaked brick; they built them side by side, and so formed streets. The houses of the wealthy covered a very large extent of ground, and appear to have been provided with a courtyard in the centre, and rows of trees. Of a small house a good idea may be got from the model which is preserved in the British Museum. There are three small rooms in it on the ground floor, and a flight of steps leads through a gallery to a rectangular doorless upper chamber, in which is seated the figure of a man: in the courtyard is the figure of a woman kneading dough at a table. The doors, opening inwards, swung on pins in sockets, and were fastened by bolts or bars as well as by locks and keys, though these latter only appear in the last days of the empire. The floors were made of stone or clay, and Wilkinson thought that the roofs were supported by rafters of the date tree arranged close together.[1] The tops of the houses were frequently used by the inhabitants to take the air in the cool of the evening; hence we may decide that there was a railing round about the top of the house, to prevent a sleepy or dozing person from falling off. It will be remembered that to 'make a battlement for thy roof'[2] is a positive command laid down by Moses in the Pentateuch.

In the houses of the wealthy the walls would be beautifully sculptured and decorated, and we may conclude that the same art which rendered their tombs so brilliant with colours and so beautiful, would be used to make the interiors of their houses attractive and pleasing; and their furniture was of the richest kind. From the monuments we gather that the leading members of the aristocracy had large estates, in which their mansions stood, and upon these were kept horses, cattle, poultry, and a large number of servants. The Egyptian landlord had his stewards, who kept an account of the revenues of his lord and transacted all his business affairs. Parts of these estates were laid out as gardens with pieces of ornamental water in them, and round about were planted rows of palm trees and vines.

The principal occupation of a great part of the people of Egypt was agriculture; this being the case, we are not surprised to find that all its operations were again carried on in the fields of Elysium by the blessed dead.

[1] Wilkinson, 'Ancient Egypt,' i. p. 357.   [2] Deut. xxii. 8.

The king was the great patron of agriculture, and the figures deposited with the dead are always made with a hoe in one hand and a whip in the other. The growing of grain made Egypt rich, and the scarcity of food in countries where agriculture was less attended to would make foreigners flock there to buy corn and bread. We have already seen that Amenemḥā III. built a huge lake with sluices and canals attached in order that the country round about might be watered; and the strictest attention was paid to the rise of the Nile, on whose inundation the hopes of a good year were centred. Nilometers were established at various points, and people were told off to watch them, and to give warning if the inundation was likely to prove destructive, or, on the other hand, to announce a plenteous and prosperous season. The rising of the Nile began about the middle of June, and as the waters rose they turned from green to dark red. When the water began to go back, great care was taken to prevent it from running out of the fields, by making dykes and embankments. The water remaining behind was in a short time absorbed into the fields, and its fertilizing mud was ready for the husbandman. The ground was then broken up with plough or hoe, the seed was sprinkled in, and its treading in performed by cattle driven there for the purpose. If the height of the inundation was 16 cubits, it was well for Egypt and her people; but if only 12, a famine was the result.

The Egyptian kings kept a standing army, but made

use of mercenary troops from the earliest times. The troops were armed with bow, spear, shield, dagger, knife, axe, sling, and sword. They wore helmets and coats of armour. The shield was frequently covered with leather outside, and the hand grasped it by means of a thong. The army was divided into sections, and each section had its own standard ; kings, princes, generals, and nobles drove in chariots.

The Egyptian laws were strict, but had been made with the welfare of the country in view. The punishment of murder was death ; adultery and treason were punished by cutting off the nose of the offender, and strangling was resorted to occasionally ; while the punishment of theft was flogging.

The Egyptians lived upon the flesh of various creatures, such as the bull, goat, geese, pigeons, ducks, as well as upon cheese, milk, and certain vegetables ; while the poor would eat the lotus, papyrus, and onion freely. At table they ate with their hands or with spoons. Wine, drunk out of a shallow bowl, was a common accompaniment of a meal, and was partaken of by both sexes. The vines were supported on a series of forked sticks, and were sometimes made to extend the whole length of one side of the garden. The monuments show that there was a pool or tank of water near the vineyard, that apes or monkeys were used to gather the grapes, and that the juice was pressed from the grapes either in a bag or in a foot press. That drunkenness existed is evident from the fact that one of the tombs in Beni-Hassan repre-

sents a drunken man being carried home from a feast.
There is another drink frequently mentioned on the
monuments, and that is beer, made from the red barley.
The sepulchral tablets make the deceased pray that
cakes and jugs of beer may be brought to him in the
nether world ; hence we may gather that it was much
esteemed in Egypt.

The Egyptians were passionately fond of hunting, and
the animals hunted were the hyæna, the gazelle, the
crocodile, and the hippopotamus ; the first two were either
shot with bow and arrows, or noosed, and the last were
speared. Birds were caught in a trap made of network, or
with a fowling stick ; and fish were caught with the rod
and line or speared.

CHAPTER XI.

ARCHITECTURE AND ART.

IN architecture the Egyptians have made to themselves a name which will last as long as the world
endures. The pyramids, which belong to a period of
more than three thousand years before Christ, are
familiar to all, and they were justly ranked among the
seven wonders of the world. Closely following on these
wonderful buildings come the sternly beautiful temples;
and from these we see that the Egyptians were perfect
masters of architectural design and detail, and also of
the knowledge of the means for cutting, polishing, and
hoisting to a great height immense masses of granite
weighing many hundreds of tons. The temples of the
gods, the obelisks recording victories and glories
achieved, and the pyramid tombs, were meet objects
on which to display their science of building, which
every succeeding generation has admired, and vainly
tried to imitate.

The principal periods of Egyptian architecture and art
are as follows :—

1. Under the kings of the fourth, fifth, and sixth
dynasties the most handsome and majestic edifices

were built, such as the pyramids and mastabas, or tombs.
The former we have referred to under the reigns of the
kings who built them, and the latter we described on
page 150.   If nothing else but these monuments
remained to us of the works of art of this period, we
should be compelled to admit that the Egyptians of
those times were mighty builders.   But fortunately we
have other remains of the work of the people of those
days, in the shape of beautifully executed statues ; from
which we see that the artist not only meant to produce
a statue and likeness, but succeeded in giving to its
features a true likeness of the man.   The most remarkable statues of this class are those of Chephren, the
third king of the fourth dynasty, and the builder of the
second pyramid, and that of the ' chief of the village,'
which are preserved in the Boulak Museum in Egypt.
In these statues nature has been copied carefully
and accurately ; and spectators who are accustomed
to the sight of the later conventional Egyptian art, are
surprised into admiration when they see before them
figures whose features are evidently ' speaking likenesses '
of the inhabitants of the Nile valley more than
five thousand years ago.   With the death of the last
king of the sixth dynasty this remarkable style of art
drooped, and eventually disappeared ; a long period of
artistic inactivity then followed, until the eleventh or
twelfth dynasty, when Egyptian art burst forth into a
new life.

II. The most remarkable productions of the second

period of Egyptian architecture and art are the obelisks
of Heliopolis, upon which in later days Joseph must
have looked ; and the rock tombs of Beni-Hassan,
scenes from which are described on page 64. In
these tombs windows and pillars are introduced, and the
scenes portrayed on the walls are invaluable for the
insight they give us into the manners and customs of
the Egyptians, their festivals, and their manufacturing
operations. The workmen and artists of this period did
not produce such life-like works as those of the earlier
periods, but were tied down by a rigid conventionality,
which destroyed the independence and freedom of their
designs, and fettered the simple grandeur of their productions. Following close upon this revival of art
under the eleventh and twelfth dynasties, came a second
period of oblivion, caused by the subjugation of Egypt
by the Shepherd Kings, when not only were no works of
art or important edifices built, but the first few of these
rulers are thought to have destroyed the beautiful
monuments of the kings of the first empire. Egyptian
art did not absolutely decline under these rulers, but it
seems to have existed in a desultory and stagnant
fashion ; and, as we should expect, to these rough, and
compared to the Egyptian, uncouth, despots, art and
architecture were of secondary importance.

III. The third period begins with the expulsion of
the Hyksos and the accession of Amāsis, the first king
of the eighteenth dynasty, about 1700 B.C. The art
of this period culminated under Rameses II., the

oppressor of the Israelites. His father, Seti I., had drawn largely upon the services of the architects, the artists and the labourers, in order to design and build magnificent and mighty temples, and to cover them with scenes and inscriptions commemorative of his battles and exploits. Under the rule of Rameses II, the most beautiful artistic works were executed ; and the oppressor king, with the assistance of myriads of captives and legions of Egyptians, erected some of the largest and best-proportioned edifices which the world has ever seen. After the reign of Rameses II. art and architecture again declined, and but little good work was produced until the twenty-sixth dynasty, about 666 B.C.

IV. Under the twenty-sixth dynasty, inaugurated by Psammetichus I., there again appeared delicately wrought buildings and elegant works of art. The Egyptian architects ·and artists went so far in their imitation of the works of past dynasties, as to reproduce on their tombs the texts which were inscribed upon the tombs of the fifth and sixth dynasties, nearly three thousand years before.

V. The fifth and last stage in Egyptian architecture and art is that which flourished under the Ptolemies. These rulers made use of the native Egyptian skill in building and decorating to a wonderful extent ; but it is easy to see that the artists of that time only *copied* what had gone before, merely keeping up the traditional letter, while the spirit of the work was long since dead. The knowledge of the old hieroglyphic language died out many years before the Ptolemies, and many of the characters had new and different values given to them under their rule. Besides this, since the national characteristics of the Egyptian race, their religion, and manners, and customs had been all changed under the new rulers, how could the art and architecture of the old and middle empires survive? Changes came on swiftly and surely, and the Egyptians hastened to welcome and adopt the wonderfully beautiful art of the Greeks.

As the Egyptian believed that his soul and the gods lived for ever, his first care was that his tomb and his temples should be everlasting. Keeping this in mind, he built them carefully and well, and of the best materials; they bear upon them the impress of edifices constructed for eternity, and not for time. The Egyptian delighted in forming massive buildings and colossi, but he was also able to build light and elegant buildings suitable for the residences of his Pharaohs. He understood the use of the arch, he was thoroughly familiar with the importance of pillars and columns, he excelled in working the hardest stone, he built everlasting structures, and he remains almost without equal in his skill in decorating walls.

And finally, the Egyptian was an expert and skilful manufacturer, a wonderful worker in gold and precious stones, and an expert weaver in linen : he was a keen and enterprising trader, and apparently exceedingly ready to take advantage of the foreign merchant. He disliked

N

the foreigner, but when it was to his advantage to
tolerate him, he did so, and was willing to accord to
him due honour for his services, as in the parallel cases
of Joseph and Saneha, 'the child of the sycamore.' As
a rule he was obedient to authority, and under good
generals fought well and did mighty deeds. He was
learned, witty, sarcastic, and devoted to the arts and
sciences, good-tempered, and of a light and happy dis-
position. He was self-sufficient, inclined to be despotic,
and it was not a difficult matter to corrupt him by a
luxurious life, of which in the days of the greatness and
wealth of the empire he was exceedingly fond. From
the earliest times he appears to have had a plurality of
gods, and he was both religious and superstitious; he
had an exceedingly high moral ideal, and a most
sublime conception of the unity of the great God and
Creator of the world. In short, he possessed all the
virtues and lofty and great ideas which were attainable
by the people of such a civilized nation as his own : he
likewise practised all the vices which spring up under the
fostering influence of luxury and wealth. Though the
knowledge of the Almighty was brought face to face
with him, he refused to learn of Him, and accounted
Him as one of his own gods; therefore, like every
nation that has raised its hand to persecute God's chosen
people, he has passed away, and his monuments alone
remain to tell us how great was the empire of the ' Sons
of the Sun ' in the valley of the Nile.

APPENDIX.

THE EGYPTIAN CALENDAR.

Egyptian Name.	Meaning.	Civil Year.	In the Sacred Year the Month begins	In the Alexandrian year the Month begins
	1st month of Spring	Thoth	July 25	August 29.
	2nd ,, ,,	Paophi	August 19	September 28.
	3rd ,, ,,	Athyr	September 18	October 28.
	4th ,, ,,	Choiak	October 18	November 27.
	1st ,, Summer or Ploughing Season	Tybi	November 17	December 27.
	2nd ,,	Mechir	December 17	January 26.
	3rd ,,	Phamenoth	January 16	February 25.
	4th ,,	Pharmuthi	February 15	March 27.
	1st ,, Inundation	Pachons	March 17	April 26.
	2nd ,,	Payni	April 16	May 26.
	3rd ,,	Epiphi	May 16	June 25.
	4th ,,	Mesore	June 15	July 25.

INDEX.

LIST OF SCRIPTURE REFERENCES.

HARRISON & SONS, Printers in Ordinary to Her Majesty, St. Martin's Lane.

www.ingramcontent.com/pod-product-compliance
Lightning Source LLC
Chambersburg PA
CBHW030830270326
41928CB00007B/982